ELIZABETH WONG

VEGETABLE COOKERY

THE CHINESE WAY

C&H CHILD & HENRY

To my Mother who taught me to love vegetables.

Published by
Child & Henry Publishing Pty Ltd
9 Clearview Place Brookvale, NSW, Australia, 2100
First Edition, 1985

Typeset by Walter Deblaere and Associates
Printed by Colourwork Press Pte Ltd,
21 Mandai Estate, Singapore
National Library of Australia Card Number and
ISBN 0 86777 113 5

Jade Salad

Contents

Foreword

Through thousands of years cookery in China has evolved to a fine art, a matter of grace and pleasure. The finest food, like the best in every art, is simply a matter of excellence in the preparation, imagination and presentation. Centuries before Western countries had discovered the dietetic merits of quick-cooked vegetables and of blending tastes, textures and colours to produce appetising and nutritious foods, the Chinese had adopted these things as essential principles of cookery.

I have had the pleasure of knowing, and the honour of working with Ella-Mei for a quarter of a century, firstly as one of her students at the Food School, East Sydney Technical College, and subsequently as a contemporary in the field of teaching. Ella-Mei is not only an authority and specialist in Chinese cookery but also a very talented author of many successful books. She has a rare gift for simple easy-to-follow explanations and a keen artist's eye in choosing those compositions to photograph which best show the completed dishes.

A work of art is always an adventure, particularly in preparing and enjoying food. For those who wish to enhance their knowledge, health and skills in a creative cuisine, I recommend *Vegetable Cookery – The Chinese Way*.

F.M. Roberts, Dip.Ed.Admin.,
Deputy Principal,
North Sydney Technical College.

Acknowledgements

My sincere thanks to Dalys Newman who also worked with me on the *Genuine Chinese Cookbook* for her valuable understanding of the works, and for the rapport that developed between us. Also to my colleague and great friend, Douglas Marsland who is always ready with assistance – his 'hands' appear in the step-by-step photographs.

As always, thanks to Kum Cheng for calligraphy.

Introduction

For centuries the Chinese have known the value of vegetables in their diet and include them in every meal; either in soup, served separately or combined with other foods. Recently, it seems to me, judging from the emergence of vegetarian food outlets and cookbooks, everyone else has suddenly discovered fresh vegetables.

The Chinese farmer is an expert in his profession and when he came overseas to work in the market gardens, returning after one year to visit his family, he introduced some of the wonderful unfamiliar vegetables that we enjoy today. He used to sell his produce by going door-to-door and was always known as 'Johnny'. What a joy it was to receive a jar of ginger in syrup at Christmas time for being such a good customer and friend.

Today, Chinese vegetables are becoming more plentiful and readily obtainable at the larger supermarkets. You can enjoy an enviable reputation for being a good cook by knowing your vegetables and how to cook them to advantage. Be critical when marketing and insist on the freshest young and tender vegetables. The secret of a good dish is using the youngest and tenderest vegetables, cooked quickly with the smallest amount of water, ensuring that the vitamin and mineral content is retained, as well as shape and texture. A good idea is to have a stock pot ready, to which you can add the vegetable off-cuts to enrich it, thus making an excellent base for soups and sauces.

On a recent visit to China, my group had the opportunity of visiting an agricultural commune in Shanghai. After the necessary welcome and greetings were exchanged (all groups are received this way) we were ushered into the board room where the principals served us with tea and told us about the production of that particular area. We were then shown the experimental division in which every conceivable vegetable was growing in large glass containers about 1 metre high. Large vegetables, such as pumpkins, cucumbers and tomatoes, were happily growing in this environment. As it was the season for beans they were growing outside on trestle-trees, and capsicums and Chinese cabbage were harvested ready for market. We also saw cattle which had been imported from Australia and were being kept to supply dairy products. The commune was complete in itself with its own housing development, school, workshop and free range ducks, chicken and pigs. We were completely impressed with the PA system and orderliness of the whole area.

There is no need to be a strict vegetarian – in fact there is no need to diet if you choose sensibly and follow my Chinese diet. When combining vegetables with meat, always plan for three parts vegetables (liquid and fibre) to two parts meat (protein) – the Yin and Yang of life. If you have ever wondered why the Chinese race is not fat, or why their skin is usually clear and of a fine texture, their hair and nails strong, this is due to this diet; lots of soy bean products, green vegetables, fruit, products from the sea, and clear hot Chinese tea. This can happen to you too.

Good Health!

ELLA-MEI WONG

Know Your Vegetables

The everyday vegetables that you are familiar with and the more unusual vegetables which I have photographed for identification will give you a repertoire worthy of any gourmand.
The Chinese chef is very particular about the method of cooking vegetables and insists that they must be only just cooked and still retain their colour and texture. They are hardly ever eaten raw but are added to hot soup, and steamed, stir-fried, braised or boiled. When using as a salad vegetable always toss in a vinaigrette dressing as the acid in the vinegar or lemon juice 'cooks' the vegetable.

If there is need to substitute a vegetable that is in the recipe for an everyday one, endeavour to choose types of the same texture (e.g. celery instead of bamboo shoots, potatoes instead of taro root or sweet potatoes, green cabbage instead of Chinese leafy vegetables).

Chinese White Cabbage

Bark Choy 白菜

This vegetable is possibly the best known of the more unusual vegetables that the Chinese use in their dishes, probably due to supply (it is available all year round), and the fact that it it harmonises with all other ingredients. The taste is sweet and succulent because of its water content and its volume is reduced considerably in its short cooking period.

Identify this vegetable by its fresh, light green, tender leaves with white stalks and white veins. When the vegetable is plentiful (summer months) it is dried (choy gone), stored in a dry place and used for flavouring soups.

To prepare the vegetable for cooking, trim off the base and make sure you wash in between the stem at the base by rubbing with your fingers to remove any soil that may remain.

Separate the green leaves from the white stalk and cook the stalks separately as they take a little longer to become tender – they may need to be peeled on the outside to remove hard strings. The taste is enhanced by adding fresh green ginger during the cooking.

Wash the green leaves thoroughly and soak in cool water for 20 minutes – it is wonderful to see what this does to the vegetable: the stalks crisp up and the green leaves blossom out to their fullest extent. The green leaves can be used raw, e.g. in Jade Salad (recipe p33) or can be sliced and used in stir-fry dishes or in soups.

Pumpkin in Black Bean Sauce (p31), Bean Sprout Noodles (p39) surrounded by Mermaid Tresses (p26), Lotus Soup (p42) and Creamed Tiensin Cabbage (p25).

Tiensin Cabbage

Wong Ah Bark 黄芽白

Also known as celery cabbage. It is a rather large vegetable with tightly wrapped pale green leaves with broad white stems. It is extremely economical to use as it can be wrapped in a plastic bag and stored for one week in the refrigerator. It can be cooked or used raw in salads. It has a delicate sweet flavour and blends well with all other ingredients. When finely sliced it is used as the base for the classic spring roll.

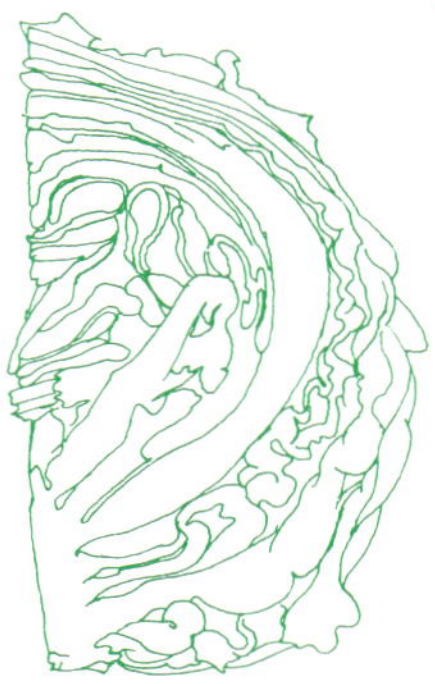

Ordinary Head Cabbage

Yeah Choy 椰菜

This large, round cabbage with tight-fitting leaves is economical and nutritious and can be eaten raw or cooked. When picked from the garden, the outer leaves are dark green and coarser in texture. When the cabbage is stored for some time, say one week, the inner leaves become very pale, almost white in colour, but are tender. Choose one that is firm and solid. This cabbage is substituted for the other types of vegetables in the Chinese cuisine because of its availability, versatility and price. It can be used for soups, boiled, braised, pickled, stuffed, chopped finely for salads and used as a filling for spring rolls.

There is also a red cabbage which can be used the same way. It exudes a reddish liquid when cooked and is excellent in soup. Also used for pickling. The Chinese way of stir-frying cabbage with a little vegetable oil, garlic and ginger makes this an appetising vegetable dish.

Another variety of cabbage, savoy cabbage – has crinkled green leaves and can be used in the same way as ordinary head cabbage.

Fresh Mustard Cabbage

Gai Choy 芥菜

This dark green leaf vegetable with firm, pale green, grooved stalks has a slight mustard flavour, thus the name mustard cabbage. Whole stems vary in size. Prepare by rinsing between stalk and stem and rubbing with the fingers to remove any surplus soil. The fresh vegetable is usually cut in sections and used in soup. When fermented for 4-5 days it is known as sin choy and is stir-fried on its own or combined with meats. See p27.

Chinese Spinach

Een Choy 莧菜

There are two types of this family; a purely green-leafed variety, and one with red tints amongst the green leaves. Foliage varies in size and the tap root must always be removed before using it as it is very tough. The plant has to be washed carefully and thoroughly as it seems to gather more soil through its long roots.

To prepare for cooking, cut off any hard stem and when washed, drain well. The leaves do not take long to cook, only a few minutes to become soft and for the volume to reduce considerably. The stems take a little longer to soften.

It can be used in soup, the red leaves giving the soup a red colour (like a beetroot soup), steamed as a side vegetable, used in a spinach pie or rolled in beef or pork mince (recipe p62).

Chinese spinach will deteriorate within one day, especially in the summer months, so it is best to use it imemdiately. Any dampness in the leaves tends to rot the vegetable in a short time. If it is not convenient to use it immediately, just place the vegetable in a small container with enough water to wet the roots and leave in a cool part of the kitchen or place straightaway in a plastic bag into the crisper. Wash and prepare the next day.

Chinese Spinach

Bor Choy 菠菜

A large, green-leafed vegetable, very delicate in appearance and taste. The volume is reduced considerably when cooked and only needs a short time to limp and cook. It is used extensively in all kinds of dishes, as a base for the main ingredients, noodle dishes, both soup and braised; soup or on its own as an independent vegetable.

As it takes such a short time to cook – under five minutes – it is an easy vegetable for the busy housewife.

To prepare: separate firmer stems from the leafy part and rinse thoroughly, removing any garden soil that may be left between the stems. Cut into 5 cm (2 in) lengths and stir-fry in vegetable oil with fresh green ginger until limp. Sprinkle with soy sauce and glisten with sesame oil or sesame-soy. Add a little water if too dry, although it will exude its own liquid.

Water Spinach

Oong Choy 蕹菜

Water spinach has triangular-shaped, pale green leaves and long, hollow stems. This vegetable has a high water content so must be used immediately. If allowed to keep for even one day the leaves tend to yellow and the stems get soggy and rot.

Separate the stems from the green foliage and discard any of the tougher stems at the bottom where there are any roots. It is used in braised dishes and soup, and the Cantonese have created a classic dish by using shrimp paste to complement this vegetable. See photograph of how to prepare, (p35).

Chinese Broccoli

Gai Larn 芥蘭

This vegetable has a hard stem similar to the ordinary type of broccoli stem and its leaves are firmer but misty green in colour, as if touched by the snow to give it that distinctive look. The mature plant sprouts white-budded flowers which are edible. The stems need to be peeled to remove the outer fibre, and then cut obliquely to facilitate cooking. I find the easiest way to prepare this vegetable is to cut the tip off the bottom and then snip off the fibres. Then use a vegetable peeler to remove the other outer fibres. The stems need to be boiled in water to tenderise. Use the liquid that remains for stock to make sauces or soup. Stir-fry the cooked stems in a little hot seasoned oil (ginger and garlic added) to just glisten, then add to other ingredients in the dish. I suggest you use only the young foliage and buds for cooking, the outer leaves are very tough in texture and need to be boiled longer to soften. The best eating parts of this vegetable are the stems and inner young hearts.

Chinese Flowering Vegetable

Choy Sum 菜心

The stems and leaves are jade green in colour and the stems are curved. The younger plants are the best for eating because when cooked they are tender and stringless. When mature, there is a small cluster of edible yellow flowers which makes the vegetable easily distinguishable. Make sure to wash betweeen the grooves of this vegetable as garden soil is often lodged between the stalks. When cooked the Chinese way the vegetable becomes a vivid green and the stems are delicately sweet and fresh to the palate.

Separate the stems from the green leaves as the leaves will lake less time to cook and limp. As this vegetable is so popular with the Chinese and does not have an overpowering flavour, it is used with all other ingredients – seafood, meats, poultry and noodle dishes. It can even be prepared as a side vegetable on its own with a few slices of fresh green ginger, soy sauce and a sprinkling of sesame and soy oils to brighten and glisten.

Chrysanthemum Vegetable

Tong Oong Choy 茼蒿菜

As the name implies, this edible vegetable has a chrysanthemum flavour. The smaller bunches are the finest for eating purposes. The leaves are a bright green with whitish veins and when mature a small chrysanthemum bud appears, which is also edible. This vegetable cooks down very quickly and the quantity reduces to one quarter in bulk, so you need to use at least one bunch with other meats (added for extra flavour) for 4 serves.

There are three known varieties of edible chrysanthemum vegetables. Two types are cultivated for use as a vegetable and the third is grown for the flower petals which are used as a garnish. Other varieties are cultivated for flowers and ornamental floral art.

In the cold winter months Chinese men find warmth and sustenance from a dish called the Three Kinds of Snake (Sarm See Saik). Snakes are especially bred for food value and aphrodisiac properties and chrysanthemum flowers are used as an important part of this dish, along with pine leaves.

This vegetable only takes a very short cooking time so is ideal for Dah Bin Loo, Steam Boat or Mongolian firepot. The chrysanthemem petals are also added to tea, making a cooling tea, very beneficial to one's system according to Chinese belief.

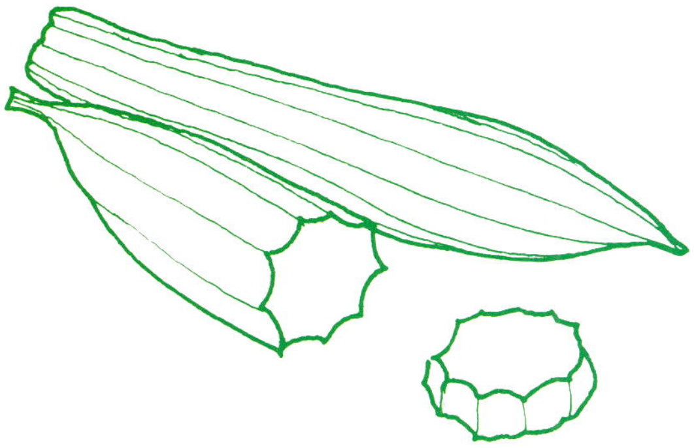

Sponge Gourd (Luffa)

See Gwah 絲瓜

This gourd is similar to a green cucumber but has distinct ridges about 1 cm (½ in) wide – these ridges are very tough especially in mature gourds. Peel off all the green skin – the creamy white flesh inside is soft and spongy. Cut the vegetable into large pieces and use in soup or stir-fry dishes. It has a deliciously sweet flavour.

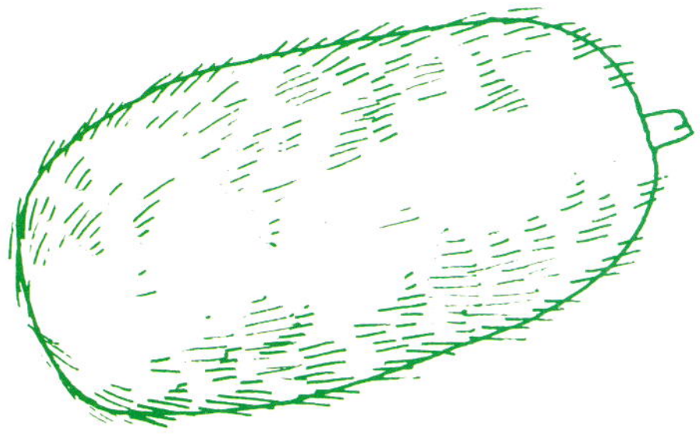

Summer Melon

Jit Gwah 節瓜

A medium-sized melon available during summer months. There is a very fine covering of tiny white fuzz on the pale green skin and the flesh inside is white with white spongy seeds.

The outer skin is rather firm and when cut away the flesh can be cut in all kinds of shapes, matchstick, diced and sliced. It can be steamed, braised or stir-fried, and when combined with other ingredients it quickly absorbs other flavours. It is also candied and served as a sweet and can be used in the making of desserts.

To store successfully: place a piece of plastic wrap over the cut portion and place melon in the crisper in your refrigerator. It will keep successfully for 1 week. In photo, p47, summer melon is used in a classic dish with cellophane noodles and crab omelette.

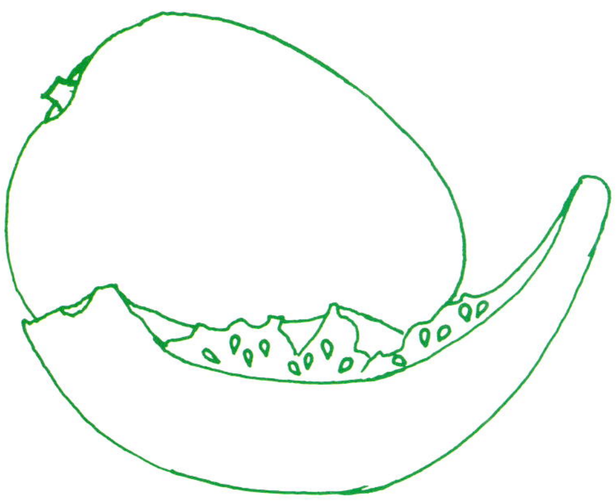

Chinese Winter Melon

Doong Gwah 冬瓜

This is available in the winter months. It is very large and the shape varies from round to long. Its skin is a pale to dark green colour and as hard as the skin of a watermelon. The flesh inside is creamy white when cooked and very tender. Doong Gwah Joong is a gourmet Chinese soup included in a gala banquet because it can be lavishly carved on the outside, thus making it a stunning centrepiece. The soup is made of cut-up melon flesh, simmered with nuts, meats and vegetables then served inside the melon. Minced ham is sprinkled on top.

The winter melon is very hardy and I have known it to last up to 4 months in a cool place in the larder. When cut, place plastic wrap over the cut surface and store in the crisper in the refrigerator. Lasts at least a week. See photograph p45.

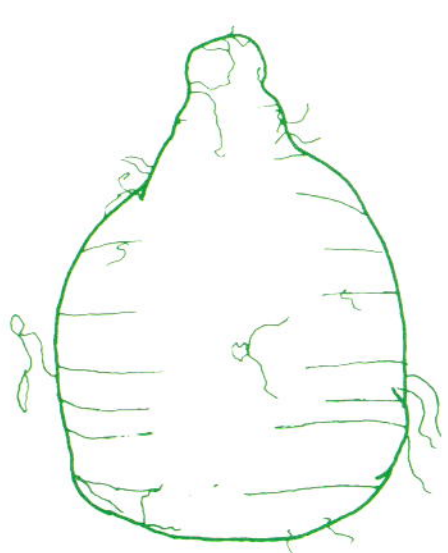

Taro

Woo Tow 芋頭

Taro is cultivated throughout the tropics for its edible tuberous rhizomes. There are two main types, one of which is similar to the sweet potato and the other type is like a small round potato. The former is best for Chinese dishes. Peel off the brownish-red skin and the inside flesh is creamy to dark reddish-brown and must be cooked to be considered safe for eating. They are very nutritious, containing valuable proteins and minerals. They are sticky when cut, so soak in cool water until ready to be cooked. They are versatile in that they can be cooked then baked, purèed, deep-fried, braised, boiled or mashed.

Lotus

Lin Kno 蓮藕

Every part of this exotic plant is used. The rhizomes are cooked with other foods to impart a unique flavour. The root itself is long, tapers to nothing and is joined together like a large sausage. It has its own natural perforations running through its entire length, and when cut it forms an unusually attractive pattern. The nuts (lin jee), are puréed and used as a nut paste, also available in cans. They are used as a filling in sweet cakes and pastries and were formerly only made for festive occasions but today are included in the yum cha collection of goodies. Lotus flour, used as a thickening agent, is also made from the nut.

The Chinese, ever superstitious, regard the lotus as a symbol of fertility. The stamens are dried and used in braised and steamed dishes. The dried long leaves are used for wrapping food, e.g. Joong, and impart a delicate flavour to the enclosed food. The canned variety is easy to use as it is already cooked and may be added straight from the can to other foods. It also comes in a dehydrated form and this is best for lotus soup. It is also candied for the New Year. If available fresh, it is peeled and cut into chunks or slices before using and has a strange stringiness when cut. It has to be cooked until tender.

Water Chestnuts

Mar Tay 馬蹄

These tiny reddish-black bulbs (similar in size to a gladioli bulb) must be peeled to reveal a creamy fruit which is sweet and crisp. The fresh ones, naturally, are desirable, but if unobtainable, they can be purchased in cans in oriental supermarkets. They give an added texture when combined with other foods. Keep covered with water and they will store in your refrigerator for 2-3 days.

They can be eaten raw or cooked, combined with all meats and vegetables and fruits. They are extremely versatile as they can be sliced, diced, minced and crushed and made into water chestnut powder.

Spring Onions

Choong 葱

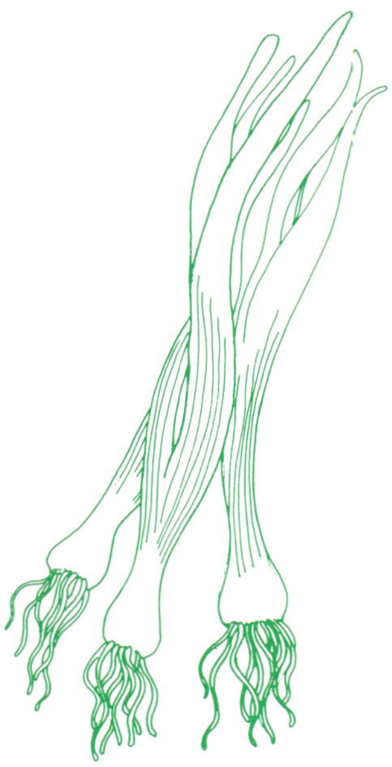

Also known as shallots, scallions or green onions. The long green stems are hollow, like a tube, and have a small white onion-like bulb attached. Some healthy plants are quite long (40 cm) but the smaller and tighter tube-like ones are most appreciated by the Chinese and are called 'winter' choong because they are grown in the winter months.

To prepare: take off the outer green stems, cut away the roots and wash and dry thoroughly. Cut into desired lengths, or dice as required. Spring onions are used in all types of dishes; rice, beef, noodles and omelettes. They are also used extensively as a garnish; cut into 2.5 cm (1 in) lengths and with a very sharp knife split the ends then place in cool water. The ends will fan out to produce a shallot flower. They can also be used as a brush; take a 10 cm (4 in) length from the shallot with the roots attached, wash thoroughly and use as a brush to spread soy bean pastes or flavourings on to a whole chicken, duck or pork.

When the onion-like bulb is allowed to mature it is pickled and is found in sweet-sour pickles. It is called choong tau, meaning 'shallot head'. There are different types of choong tau which are sold in clusters and vary in colour from brown-red to purple-red. In Asian countries, if you ask for shallots, these are the bulbs you would receive. Their taste is stronger than the ordinary onion and they are used extensively in all dishes, imparting a glorious flavour. They can be deep-fried, crushed, minced, braised and crushed and used in marinades, and they make steamed or stir-fry dishes a gourmet's delight.

Snow Peas

Hollan Doe

These edible pea pods are flat with a tiny bulge where the immature peas are enclosed. The smaller variety are the most desirable as they are crisper, sweeter and more tender. They can be used in any combination of foods and are especially delectable when stir-fried with fresh green ginger, garlic and oil.

To prepare: string the pea pod from top to bottom down one side, then string the other side from bottom to top.

Snow Pea Tendrils

Dow Miu 豆苗

Not many people are aware of the fact that the snow pea vine is used as a vegetable nor have they ever tasted the foliage. This is probably because the plant is prevented from flowering and producing snow peas, so it becomes scarce and expensive. It is only used for special occasions and because the tendrils are so tender and immature it is believed that the properties of the Fountain of Youth will remain with the diner.

The foliage should be used on the same day that it is picked, washed and left in cool water to refresh before using. It is used in soup, needing only a short time to soften in the hot stock, and also used as a vegetable combined with other foods.

Bean Sprouts

Knar Choy 芽菜

Fresh bean sprouts are sprouted from mung beans, tiny green-coloured round beans. Try sprouting them yourself a few at a time by soaking a handful in warm water to burst the skin, then place on a muslin cloth spread over a colander, place in a dark corner, or cover lightly with a lid, and water each day. Allow the water to rinse through. In 4-5 days, you will have bean sprouts for your salad. Today, with new technology, there is a machine which sprouts the beans automatically and is certainly more expedient than the old method of having a room which had water running through the floor in gutter form to rinse the beans while maturing, and required someone to attend 24 hours a day to adjust the temperatures to produce first-class merchandise.

They are high in nutrition and inexpensive to buy. They add a crunchy texture to salads, can be used in all types of dishes, and are excellent in Spring Rolls.

When purchased fresh, put them in a bowl of cool water and any skin left clinging to the mung bean will wash off. Keep them in water until ready for use as they will remain plump and fresh. Try to use them in one day, if not, stand in water in the refrigerator for another day. I do not recommend keeping them any longer.

They are also available in cans, but have lost their crunchiness and plumpness by this procedure.

Soy Bean Sprouts

Dai Dow Knar Choy 大豆芽菜

These sprouts are larger than their younger brother, the mung bean sprout. They have a larger, golden-coloured bean at one end, about 1 cm long, that tends to dislodge itself during cooking. Soy bean sprouts are one of the most nutritious foods available – they have a large amount of protein and vitamin C and their nutritional value is equivalent to that of meat and eggs. They are economical, crunchy and have a slightly nutty flavour.

To store soy bean sprouts, leave them in a plastic bag in the crisper of your refrigerator and they will keep up to 3 days. Always blanch them before using if adding to salad greens, or cook them as directed in the recipe. They are not as tender as mung bean sprouts.

Chives

Gow Choy, Gow Wong, Gow Choy Farr

Chives uplift any dish by their flavour and texture. They are easily grown in pots and thrive in the garden. They grow from bulbs and propagate themselves from the bulb, each bulb growing into another plant.

Gow Choy 韮菜

Long flat green leaves, available in bunches, without the roots. They have a slightly stronger flavour than shallots, but their texture is a little tougher. The shorter lengths are naturally younger, more tender and more delicate in flavour. Chives lend themselves beautifully to omelettes and are also used in salads, soups, stir-fried, braised and steamed dishes. When fully matured the flower is purple.

Gow Wong

Same as above only they are grown in dark glass-houses which eliminate the formation of chlorophyll, with the result that the leaves are pale yellow in colour. They should be used immediately as they are extremely delicate and keeping qualitites are limited to one day. These chives are best used sprinkled on top of noodles, in salads and quickly stir-fried dishes.

Gow Choy Farr 韮菜花

These chives have long round stems with a bud on each tip and are considered good eating at this stage. When the bud opens to a flower they are considered too tough to eat. The taste is similar to onions, and they can be used in salads, omelettes or soups. The Chinese use them as a substitute for shallots in stir-fry dishes with beef, chicken and seafood. All types of gow choy are also braised with bean curd.

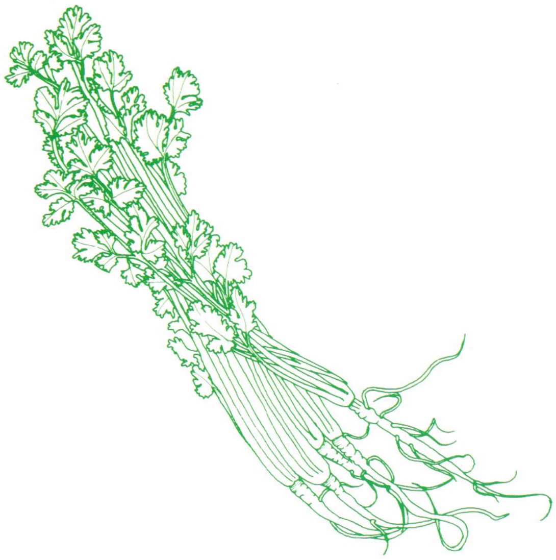

Coriander (Chinese Parsley)

Yin Say 芫茜

The best type of fresh coriander is that with small delicate green leaves on a small spray with a tapering root. Scrub the roots well to remove garden soil and use in stocks for soups. Coriander has an unusual, pleasant scent and is harmonious with all types of other foods and vegetables, cooked or uncooked. Use the same way as ordinary parsley. It is easily grown by seed and these can also be used in recipes for curries and casseroles. It deteriorates very quickly so store the unwashed plants in a plastic bag in the crisper of your refrigerator. Keep in cool water to refresh.

Watercress

Say Yeung Choy 西洋菜

These bundles of small green leaves attached to a hollow stem usually have small white roots attached at intersections. The long stems are separated from the young green sprigs and boiled down until all the flavour is extracted and the resulting liquid is used in soup. The young green sprigs are stir-fried lightly in vegetable oils, sprinkled with soy sauce and used as a side vegetable or as a base for the main dish. Can also be used in salads or for decoration. Use watercress quickly as it tends to rot if left out of water for too long.

Cooking The Chinese Way In Your Kitchen

Mastering Cookery Methods

Stir Fry (Chow)

The only new cookery method you need to master is chow (stir-fry). With the knowledge you already have of boiling, frying, simmering, baking, deep-frying, casserole cooking, grilling and barbecuing, you will be able to produce every recipe in this book.

Chow, literally translated, means 'to fry' – to fry in very little oil, in a little more oil, or dry-fry, as opposed to deep-fry, where the ingredients need to be fully immersed in the oil. You can work out for yourself what to expect when studying a Chinese menu from Chow Farn (fried rice); Chow Mein (fried noodles) or Chow Kno Yuk Farn (fried meat with rice). Stir-frying accounts for most of the dishes in Chinese restaurants because it is quick and economical, which is a very important factor in running a restaurant. It also enables the cook to show his expertise by a harmonious blending of both meats and vegetables held together by natural juices – a little stock is added to make a subtle sauce, which can be thickened slightly. Chinese wine is sprinkled over the dish for extra flavour, and the hot dish is ready at the table in under ten minutes.

Learn the secret of chow and do it with style. Just observe the following rules and you are an expert in cooking Chinese food: Always heat the wok or frying pan to the point that a drop of water will sizzle. Add your cooking oil to heat, then add fresh green ginger and garlic whose flavours will be absorbed in the oil, then chow (stir-fry) your meat and vegetables and add stock and seasonings.

Steaming (Jing)

You will find that steaming (jing) is another cooking method you will use time and time again, especially if you like nutritious and tasty dishes. You can also steam the dish to reheat (it can be cooked beforehand). Heat the rice, make a salad, and you have produced a wholesome and nutritious meal in a very short time. The Chinese steam fish, egg, vegetables and minced meats in an open dish in a deep saucepan. Start off with hot water in the wok or saucepan, stand a trivet or upturned empty can or basin in the water, place your dish to be steamed on this but do not allow it to touch the sides of the saucepan (this is to enable the steam to circulate around and over the dish).

The water must come below the dish to be cooked otherwise the water can seep into the dish of food and spoil. Cover the saucepan with a lid and steam. Left-over rice can be reheated this way very successfully. The only necessity is a deep plate or shallow basin that will fit comfortably in the wok or saucepan. Food that needs to be reheated can be placed in a number of small rice basins – four can fit snugly in a large saucepan.

Steaming (Choy)

This direct steaming or wet steaming method is applied with bamboo steamers which fit inside the wok. The wok is filled with boiling water (not touching the bottom of the bamboo steamer) and the bamboo steamer is covered with a bamboo lid. Individual serves of steamed buns, dim sims, glutinous puddings and rice cakes are cooked by this method. Larger bamboo steamers hold a whole fish, chicken and beef dishes.

Steaming (Dunn)

This is usually done in a slim earthenware casserole with a lid. Whole pieces of pork or whole chicken, pigeons with herbs and seasonings are cooked, then the casserole is placed in a larger receptacle with enough water to reach all the way up the sides of the slim casserole and steamed gently for 8 hours or more. Medicinal soup is prepared this way – the result is a brew with magical powers that brings renewed vigour to the body.

Cooking with vegetable oils

Before it was possible to purchase different brands of vegetable oils, Chinese chefs mainly used unrefined peanut oil for cooking and, in the winter months, also used lard. As the peanut oil was unrefined or 'raw' it had to be placed on the heat for a few minutes to 'cook' with the addition of fresh green ginger and garlic to give added flavour and clarify the oil. The ginger and garlic was discarded and the oil placed in a container and used when required.

In my recipes I just mention 'vegetable' oil, and this means whatever brand is your favourite, or even a mixture of all. There are peanut (refined), corn, soy, grapeseed (very expensive), walnut, sesame (used sparingly) and coconut oils. One thing you must bear in mind is that the vegetable oil must not be so strong in aroma and flavour that it overwhelms the food. Olive oil is not used in Chinese cooking as it is too overpowering. Experiment, buy different kinds of vegetable oil and stay with the one that you prefer or suits your requirements.

When using larger quantities of oil for cooking methods such as deep-frying do not discard the oil that remains. Pour the oil into a *dry* container – any residue will stay at the bottom. If you are very meticulous, strain the oil through a muslin cloth. I just strain off the residue through chopsticks and the oil is ready for use again. If you do a lot of cooking, it will be used up very quickly. *Do not* refrigerate the oil.

I always begin cooking by heating the wok first, and then adding the oil. The correct temperature is all-important; if the oil is too hot when deep-frying it will turn darker brown in colour, taste burnt and its keeping capacity will be impaired. The above method is one of the secrets of Chinese cooking. Heating the wok first ensures it is completely dry, and when the oil is added it will not splatter and food will not stick to the pan. I cannot emphasise this procedure enough.

Lard gives a completely different flavour to your dishes and should only be used in a cold climate or winter months, because when the food becomes cold (if you have any left overs) the lard congeals and is not as free-flowing as vegetable oils. In the northern parts of China, where the winter is severe, lard is used extensively. It is also used in the production of biscuits and pastries, giving an unusual crispness and very flaky texture to the finished product.

Basic Equipment

Chopsticks

These may be made of wood, bamboo, plastic, ivory, or silver. Those used for the purpose of eating are usually about 23-25 cm (9-10 in) long, and those used for cooking are longer and always made of wood. From the top, the chopsticks taper down to either a rounded or a pointed end, and this is the end used for

picking up food. Both chopsticks must be held a little higher than the middle, and both must be even. If you are not eating with chopsticks you are not eating 'Chinese'. But first you have got to get the nack.

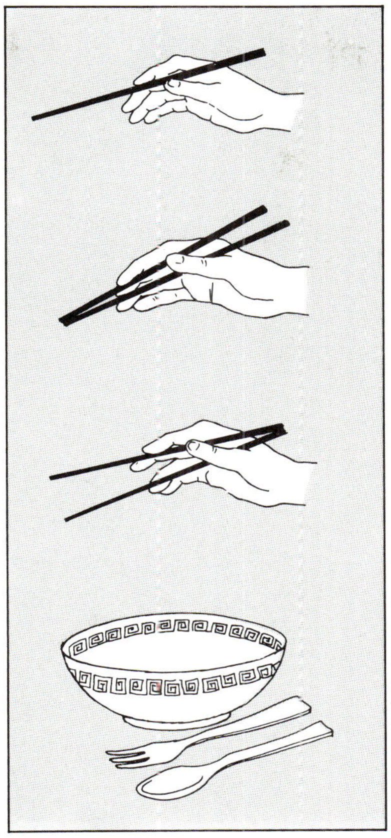

Step 1. Grasp one chopstick a little above the middle, resting under your thumb. Firmly press against middle finger.

Step 2. Put the other chopstick between the tip of thumb and index finger.

Step 3. Holding chopsticks firmly and both level, move the top one up and down keeping bottom one still.

Step 4. If you have to give up use the 'western' method and enjoy your meal just the same, with a fork and spoon. I call these 'L' learner chopsticks.

When the hold is mastered, chopsticks will do no end of kitchen chores including the beating of eggs, stirring, mixing, and piercing. Either end can be used when cooking so as not to disturb individual flavours. Chopsticks are easy to keep clean and seldom break, which makes them the most indispensable and economical of kitchen utensils.

The Chinese name for chopsticks, fai jee, means 'quick brothers', which suggests the quickness with which they can work. Each set consists of ten pairs, and it is traditional to present a Chinese girl with a set on marriage, hoping she will quickly produce lively and nimble boys.

A great breach of etiquette is to leave chopsticks crossed on the rice bowl. They are never crossed at any time, but are set parallel to each other. The Chinese, ever superstitious, feel the crossed chopsticks are a sign of evil and bad fortune.

At a formal party, a sign to commence is when the host picks up his chopsticks and invites the guests to begin. It is permissible for him to select any particular portion of food from any side of the dish to serve guests, and it is considered quite an honour to be the recipient. In Chinese family life, everyone waits until the head of the family starts before partaking of the food.

Chinese food is prepared in such a way to suit the chopsticks. A table setting consists of chopsticks, rice bowl, plate, soup bowl, porcelain spoon and a small plate for bones. The porcelain spoon reduces the heat of the soup so it will not burn the tongue. A smaller round base, which moves in a circular motion, is often placed in the centre of the round table. Known as the 'lazy susan,' it is moved around to enable everyone to make their own choice of food.

Cooking Chopsticks

Use only long *wooden* ones for cooking, and use two pairs to stir and mix, i.e. stirring rice when it is cooking. They are also excellent for draining large pieces

Stir Frying Lamb for Sizzling Mongolian Lamb (p70).

of food and tossing salad dressings, as the lemon or vinegar will not discolour the chopsticks as they would a fork.

What to cook on

It is possible to cook Chinese food on any type of heat gas and electric ranges, charcoal and electric appliances. Use a collar or ring that fits snugly around te coil of your working range, place your wok on top and it works. In some of the villages in China anything that burns, husks from the field, twigs and dried bark are used in braziers and clay pots. The expertise lies in knowing how to control the heat and apply it to the type of dish you expect to cock.

The Wok

This is the most necessary piece of equipment in Chinese cooking. A ladle (wok chan), soup ladle (tong hock) and wooden chopsticks (fai jee) are standard equipment to accompany the wok.

There have been many new types of wok on the market over the last few years; stainless steel, aluminium, copper base, wooden handles, two handles, teflon coated and flat base, but the traditional Chinese wok has not been changed for centuries. It is a thin iron, semi-circular shape with two small handles. The ideal size is 35-40 cm overall, that can serve two to six portions and is light enough to move around on the flame. If cooking on an electric coil, purchase a rim to sit the wok on top comfortably. The wok is important to Chinese food because it heats fast, and can be used for practically all the cookery methods required; stir-frying, steaming, simmering, braising, poaching and deep-frying.

Once you have seasoned your wok, you need never wash it again, as long as you take good care of it after each use. When you buy your new wok wash it out with detergent and water then rinse. Oil it lightly with fat or any vegetable oil, heat for a few minutes, rinse with hot water, dry it over a flame and it is ready for use. When cleaning it after cooking, wash out with water and bamboo brush (available in Chinese supermarkets) or scrape out any food with a Chinese ladle (wok chan), wash in hot water and dry over heat.

The electric wok

There are a number of electric woks on the market today, and for sheer convenience there is nothing more practical. Learn to know how to use your particular piece of equipment and in a short time you will become quite skilled and produce some outstanding Chinese dishes. Excellent for cooking Firepots.

Tong Hock

This is used to measure out the amount of liquid required. Half a scoop = half a cup. When the wok is heated ready for cooking, ladle your cooking oil from the tong hock in a circular movement halfway down the wok. This ensures a well-oiled wok as the wok shape lets the oil run down to the bottom.

When adding the stock and thickening ingredients, move the contents to the sides of the wok and cook in the centre. Stir the mixture with the tong hock; the ingredients will not absorb more liquid than is necessary.

The tong hock is also used to ladle hot oil on top of the finished dish to give it a sheen.

Wok chan

This is like a lifter and its three sides have a tiny rim to hold liquid when you lift the food. The bottom edge is slightly curved to use in conjunction with the curved surface of the wok.

Both the wok chan and tong hock can be used one in each hand to stir-fry the food more quickly so no part is inclined to be cooked more than the other, ensuring even distribution of heat.

Preparation and Organisation

Because a pair of chopsticks is the only eating implement (there is no knife on the table) the food must be prepared in pieces that can be easily manipulated. If food is served whole, such as steamed duck, then it is cooked so tender that it can be easily broken off with the chopsticks.

Meat is always cut across the fibres and in thin slices to make it tender. If making small cuts like 'dice' there is no need to look for the fibres, as the cuts are so small that the fibres will render themselves tender. This method of different cuts enables the same ingredient, e.g. chicken, to turn up on a menu several times in a differently cut dish, e.g. as shredded chicken, diced chicken.

When a whole chicken, duck or goose is cut up for presentation the arrangement of sections is:

back sections sliced
top and breast section sliced
thigh, wings on the side.

Ingredients may be sliced, diced, minced, cubed, crushed, shredded and marinated. The perfectionist tries to keep some kind of uniformity in the size and shape of the ingredients in a dish: e.g. if preparing a dish of pork and bean sprouts, the pork would be shredded and not cubed, because the bean sprouts are long and thin. The precise cutting of vegetables and meat ensures an attractive looking dish. The finished dish should present itself as a work of art with symmetrical proportions This uniformity also ensures that cooking time for food never varies and more importantly there is no waste.

There is maximum preparation and minimum cooking in most Chinese dishes, which is of great advantage to the housewife. Advance planning and preparation of a simple meal or feast means labour saved and ingredients can be quickly combined then bound by subtle sauces and gravies to become delicious offerings. This means there is great economy in the fuel bill and if the recipe calls for beef or pork to be marinated, then cheaper cuts can be used as they will become more tender and will absorb the full flavour of the marinade.

Planning is imperative if you want a successful Chinese meal. Have the basic ingredients - soy sauce, vegetable oils, salt and pepper, sugar and cornflour - handy to your cooking area; bean pastes, satay sauces and barbecue sauce in your refrigerator and the main ingredients already marinated, vegetables washed and cut and, in some cases, blanched, ready to be added to the dish.

Have cornflour already blended with cool water because as the cooking progresses there is no time to stop and prepare the paste as your food may overcook. The cornflour is always added at the end by making a well in the centre of the wok and stirring to thicken the liquid. Then the whole dish is stirred to absorb the sauce. A little oil is often added at this stage – along with the cornflour, it helps give the dish a lustre.

Etiquette and Serving of Food

To fully appreciate Chinese food it is desirable to have an understanding of the Chinese life style and essential to have a knowledge of etiquette.

When the family sits down for a meal all the food is placed on the table at the same time. Each person is served with a bowl of hot steaming rice and everyone waits for the head of the family to pick up his chopsticks to begin. Usually there are three or four dishes, plus soup and appetiser followed by fresh fruit and tea. When a second helping of rice is required, both hands are stretched out to receive the bowl, in fact, everything is received in such a manner.

It is a very different presentation at a formal dinner in a restaurant, when major birthdays (forty-one, fifty-one, sixty-one), weddings, anniversaries, and the birth of a child (one-month-old) are celebrated. The cost of the feast is calculated by the number of round tables of ten persons, and the menu decided upon from seven courses upwards. The sequence of dishes on a formal banquet menu remains the same. They are served in this order; cold platters (creative designs) two to four, the more lavish, nine to sixteen, light entrée dishes, the first light soup, eight or more main course dishes, second important soup, fish, noodles, dessert, and tea. Rice is usually not served, unless requested.

At birthdays, noodles in long strands and small cakes, made in the shape of a peach, representing the symbol of long life are served. A very nice custom observed at weddings is when the bridal party goes from one table to the other, drinking each other's health and in this way exchanging pleasantries with their guests.

One dish is served at a time and only a small portion given to each person as there are so many courses in a banquet menu. In between courses the guests sip tea or wine and nibble watermelon seeds. When congratulations are in order, the host and hostess move from table to table toasting the guests. No wonder it takes hours to sit through a Chinese banquet! At the end, fragrant warm towels are handed to the guests.

Dried Ingredients

Chinese food is known the world over, wherever there are Chinese communities. Dried ingredients are common in China because every family is familiar with the drying process. When there is an abundant harvest, food must be preserved and stored until next season, consequently, dried food is used as frequently as fresh or frozen food.

The dried ingredients rarely spoil even when packed to travel long distances, especially today with air transportation so frequent, and authentic Chinese dishes can be faithfully reproduced. It is often argued that an ethnic cuisine is improved outside its national boundaries.

If you are serious about your Chinese cookery and want to produce a genuine Chinese dish, use the dried ingredients that are available in Chinese stores. There you will see tall bamboo baskets full of interesting fruits and vegetables that have been dehydrated. Very little tuition is needed to learn how to prepare them.

The health-conscious Chinese believe that shark's fins, beche-de-mer, bird's nests, jellyfish, gristle, chicken feet and duck's web feet all contain animal protein. The black and silver tree fungus (chee yee) contains vegetable protein and is devoid of fat content. They are all high protein gelatinous foods which help to repair body tisue. When these foods are taken as a regular part of the diet, the Chinese believe bones and sinews will not become brittle with old age. The ingredients are purchased pre-packaged and last indefinitely.

Vegetable Dishes

Creamed Tiensin Cabbage

Wong Ah Bark

½ bunch of tiensin cabbage (wong ah bark)
4/5 cups water or vegetable stock
1 piece fresh green ginger
½ teaspoon soy sauce
1 teaspoon warm vegetable oil
½ cup cream
1 tablespoon toasted sesame seeds
tomatoes (tom thumbs) for garnish

Trim cabbage by removing thick bottom stem and discarding any outer leaves, if spoiled. Keep vegetable in one piece. Wash thoroughly by separating leaves, but do not break off. Boil water or stock in wok with ginger. Put in vegetable and cook until hard stem has softened, approximately 5-7 minutes. Lift out and drain. Place on serving platter. Sprinkle with soy sauce and vegetable oil. Pour off stock in wok, leaving half a cup. Add cream to heat through and pour over vegetable. Sprinkle with toasted sesame seeds. Garnish with miniature tomatoes (tom thumbs). See photograph below.

*Milk is used in China, although scarce, but in overseas restaurants cream is more readily available and used liberally.

Toasting sesame seeds for Creamed Tiensin Cabbage.

Creamed Tiensin Cabbage.

Steamed Chinese White Cabbage
Bark Choy

1 small bunch Chinese white cabbage (bark choy)
1 teaspoon soy sauce
1 tablespoon vegetable oil
black pepper

Separate white stalks from green leaves. Peel with a vegetable peeler to remove any tough fibres. Cut in short lengths. Wash thoroughly, especially in the grooves, and then soak in cool water for 30 minutes. Place on a saucer standing on a trivet or upturned basin and steam over boiling water for 10 minutes. Remove. Spoon over soy sauce. Heat vegetable oil and pour over the cabbage. Sprinkle with ground black pepper. Enough for 2 serves for a main course.

*For western tastes, after steaming add a knob of butter and season with salt and pepper.

Chilli Cabbage
Lart Jew Choy

½ bunch tiensin cabbage (wong ah bark)
1 tablespoon salt
2 tablespoons vegetable oil
1 piece fresh green ginger, shredded
4 hot chillies or capsicums, sliced
2 tablespoons sugar
1 teaspoon sesame-soy
3 tablespoons white vinegar
1 teaspoon soy sauce

Remove stem from bottom of cabbage and discard any soiled stalks. Cut cabbage stalks into thin slices. Wash thoroughly and place in a bowl with salt for 30 minutes. Wash and drain thoroughly. Heat wok and when hot add oil and ginger. When oil starts to sizzle, remove wok from heat and put in sliced chillies. Return to heat and stir-fry for ½ minute. Add sugar, sesame-soy, vinegar and soy sauce and mix well. Pour over the drained cabbage. Place in refrigerator to chill. The result should be sweet-sour crusty cabbage.

Stir-Fried Head Cabbage
Yeah Choy

½ head cabbage
1 piece fresh green ginger, thinly sliced
1 clove garlic, crushed
2 tablespoons vegetable oil
½ cup stock
salt
freshly ground pepper
1 teaspoon soy sauce

Cut cabbage into 2.5cm (1in) pieces. Wash thoroughly. Drain. Scrape skin from green ginger and cut into thin slices. Crush garlic. Heat wok and when hot add oil. Put in green ginger and garlic. Allow to heat through (do not brown). Then put in cabbage and stir-fry for 1 minute. Add stock and stir occasionally. Cook until tender, approximately 3-5 minutes. Season as desired. Remove garlic. Just before serving, mix in soy sauce. Serve with any juices that remain.

Mermaid Tresses
Bark Choy Mo

1 bunch Chinese white cabbage (bark choy)
oil for deep-frying
sugar

Separate green leaves from white stalks. Use white stalks in another recipe. Wash the green leaves, dry thoroughly then shred finely. Allow to stand until dry.

Heat oil in wok and when almost smoking, put in green leaves and deep-fry for a minute. The leaves should retain their colour and become crisp. Drain on absorbent paper. Sprinkle with a tiny quantity of sugar. Use as a garnish for other dishes. See photograph p8.

*Parsley can be deep-fried in this manner as well.

Pickled Mustard Cabbage

Sin Choy

500 g (1 lb) pickled mustard cabbage (sin choy)
3 tablespoons oil
1 teaspoon sugar
250 g (8 oz) topside beef
1 red sweet capsicum, diced

Soak pickled mustard cabbage in cool water to remove excess saltiness. Squeeze dry. Cut into small dice. Heat wok and when hot put in 2 tablespoons oil and stir-fry vegetable for 1 minute. Add sugar and stir for another ¼ minute. Remove to serving platter.

Chop beef into small dice. Add 1 tablespoon oil to clean wok, and when smoking, stir-fry beef until coloured. Add diced capsicum, return pickled vegetable and mix together thoroughly. Add a little water if too dry. Serve with plain boiled rice. See photograph, p49.

*This dish is served dry, the moisture remaining in the vegetable.

Chinese Spinach

Een Choy

1 bunch Chinese spinach (een choy)
2 tablespoons vegetable oil
1 teaspoon sesame oil
1 piece fresh green ginger, crushed
1 clove garlic, crushed
½ teaspoon sugar
1 teaspoon soy sauce
1 tablespoon water
2 tablespoons rose wine

Prepare vegetable by removing roots, hard stems and washing thoroughly. Drain. Heat wok and when hot add oils, green ginger and garlic. When ginger and garlic brown, remove and discard. Take wok off the heat and put in drained spinach. Return wok to heat, turn spinach over quickly with spatula. Sprinkle in sugar and soy sauce and keep turning until vegetable becomes limp. Add water if necessary (cooking will extract moisture from the spinach). Sprinkle with rose wine just before serving. Serves 4 as an extra vegetable with main meal.

Cucumber Relish

Larn Poon Wong Gwah

1 long green cucumber
¼ cup water
1 tablespoon salt
2 tablespoons white vinegar
1 teaspoon sugar
1 piece fresh green ginger, shredded
2 teaspoons vegetable oil
1 teaspoon sesame oil
1 small red chilli

Peel most of the green skin from cucumber, and cut in half lengthwise. Scoop out seeds. Cut cucumber finely in oblique slices. Place in a deep bowl with the water and salt. Allow to stand 15-20 minutes, then pour off the water and wash off the excess salt from the cucumber. Squeeze dry. Place in a salad bowl with mixture of vinegar, sugar and shredded ginger. Toss with vegetable oil and sesame oil. Decorate with strips of red chilli. Chill in refrigerator before serving.

Snow Peas

Hollan Dow

250 g (8 oz) snow peas
2 tablespoons vegetable oil
1 piece fresh green ginger, slivered
¼ cup water
½ teaspoon sugar
½ teaspoon soy sauce
¼ cup rose wine
½ teaspoon sesame-soy

Peel off the ends and any strings from snow peas. Rinse with cool water and drain. Heat wok, add oil, and when hot add slivers of ginger. Put in snow peas and stir-fry until the oil glistens the vegetable. Do not allow to brown, so reduce heat. Put in water, sugar and soy sauce and blend with snow peas until tender, but not mushy. Sprinkle with rose wine. Just before serving, pour over sesame-soy. Serve as a side vegetable with the liquid or use combined with other dishes.

*String the bean pod from top to bottom down one side then string the other side from bottom to top.

Breaking off stems of the Chinese flowering vegetable and cutting into uniform lengths.

Stalks of the Chinese Flowering Vegetable

Choy Sum

1 bunch of Chinese flowering vegetable (choy sum)
2.5 cm (1 in) piece fresh green ginger, slivered
1 tablespoon vegetable oil
3 cups vegetable stock
1 tablespoon sesame-soy
1 tablespoon soy sauce

Divide vegetable into two sections removing green leaves and keeping just the pale green stems. Break off stems and cut into uniform lengths. Wash thoroughly. Scrape off skin from fresh ginger and cut into fine slivers. Heat wok and when hot add oil and slivers of ginger. Allow oil to heat and warm ginger, do not brown. Put in stalks and stock and allow to simmer until tender, approximately 10-15 minutes. Do not cover with a lid. Replenish with more stock if necessary.

To serve, ladle stalks onto serving plate and spoon over sesame-soy and soy sauce.

*Sesame-soy is a prepared mixture of sesame oil and soy bean oil available at most oriental supermarkets.

Combined Vegetable Dish

Sub Gum Choy Woo

1 bunch green Chinese vegetable
(bark choy, gai larn)
4 cups water
2 large tomatoes, peeled and quartered
1 tablespoon sugar
1 tin straw mushrooms
1 tin baby corn
2 tablespoons vegetable oil, hot

Sauce
1 teaspoon cornflour
1 cup vegetable stock
1 teaspoon light soy sauce
1 teaspoon salt
½ teaspoon sesame oil

Cut stems of green vegetable into the same size as baby corn. Cut off any hard fibres and wash. (Reserve green tops for soup or salad.) Plunge into boiling water for 2-3 minutes. Drain, reserving liquid.

Sprinkle sugar over quartered tomatoes. Strain liquid from straw mushrooms and baby corn and add to water from the blanching of green vegetables. Bring this vegetable stock to the boil and heat tomatoes until limp, but retaining their shape. Heat mushrooms, baby corn and green stems.

Arrange all vegetables attractively on platter and spoon hot oil over green vegetables.

To make sauce: Blend cornflour with a little cold stock. Heat remainder of stock in small saucepan and cook in cornflour. Add soy sauce, salt and lastly stir in sesame oil to glisten. Pour over vegetables.

Stalks of the Chinese Flowering vegetable (above) and Steamed Rice with Spiced Meats (p64).

Chinese Broccoli

Gai Larn

1 bunch Chinese broccoli
4 cups water
1 tablespoon vegetable oil
1 piece fresh green ginger, shredded
½ cup stock (or beef bouillon cube dissolved in warm water)
1 teaspoon soy sauce
1 teaspoon sesame oil
2 tablespoons rose wine
60 g (2 oz) barbecued pork (see p63)

Wash vegetable thoroughly. Separate leaf portion from hard stem. Peel the outside fibres from the stem then cut into 4 cm (1 ¼ in) oblique slices. Retain white flowers, if any, to put with green leaves of vegetable. Boil water and cook hard stems until tender. Add green portion for 2 minutes, until wilted, then remove all to serving platter. Heat wok and when hot add oil and shredded ginger. Stir-fry vegetables for ½ minute, pour in stock, soy sauce, sesame oil and cook until heated through. Flambé with rose wine. Serve on platter with barbecued pork.

Long Beans and Water Chestnuts

Dow Gock Gar Mar Tay

½ bunch long beans (dow gock)
16 fresh water chestnuts or 1 white turnip
4 cups water
1 tablespoon vegetable oil
1 piece fresh green ginger, shredded
½ teaspoon soy sauce
salt and pepper

Cut tips from long beans and section in 8 cm (3 in) lengths. Wash and drain. Peel fresh water chestnuts and place in cool water. If using white turnips, peel and use a melon baller to cut into rounds, then cook in water until tender. Blanch long beans in hot water for 1 minute. Remove and drain. Heat wok and when hot add oil and ginger. Put in beans and keep moving in wok to glisten. Add water chestnuts or turnips, ½ cup of water (from blanching) and simmer for 1 minute. Just before serving, sprinkle with soy sauce. Add salt and pepper to taste.

Zucchini and Ginger

Ai Gwah Chow Gueng See

4-6 zucchini
2 tablespoons vegetable oil
1 teaspoon sesame oil
1 large piece fresh green ginger, shredded
½ cup stock
1 teaspoon soy sauce
1 teaspoon sesame-soy
2 tablespoons rose wine

Cut ends off zucchini, peel off most of the green skin and cut into rounds. Rinse and drain. Heat wok and when hot add vegetable oil and sesame oil and ginger. When sizzling, put in zucchini and stir-fry for ½ minute. Put in stock, soy sauce and sesame-soy. Cover with a lid and simmer for ½ minute. Just before serving, sprinkle with rose wine.

Soy Bean Sprouts

Dai Dow Knar Choy

250 g (8 oz) soy bean sprouts
2 tablespoons vegetable oil
1 teaspoon sesame oil
1 piece fresh green ginger, slivered
½ cup vegetable stock, or water
1 teaspoon soy sauce
sugar
pepper

Wash soy bean sprouts and bunch them together – keep root ends together so it is more convenient to discard all the roots at once instead of individually. Drain. Heat wok and when hot add vegetable oil and sesame oil and slivers of ginger. When almost smoking, remove wok from heat and put in drained soy bean sprouts. Return to heat and then turn over with spatula. Add vegetable stock, soy sauce and sugar and cover with a lid for 1 minute. Remove lid. Sprinkle with ground pepper and ladle sprouts and liquid onto serving plate.

Mixed Vegetables with Oyster Sauce

Sub Gum Ho Yo

60 g (2 oz) snow peas
30 g (1 oz) cloud ears (chee yee), soaked in warm water for 15 minutes
2 cups stock
1 tablespoon oyster sauce
1 teaspoon soy sauce
2 tablespoons vegetable oil
2 carrots, sliced
1 stick celery, sliced
10 water chestnuts, sliced
1 tablespoon cornflour
1 tablespoon water
1 teaspoon sesame-soy

Remove tips and any strings from snow peas. If too large cut into two sections obliquely. Wash soaked chee yee thoroughly and boil for 5 minutes in stock, oyster sauce and soy sauce. Then simmer for 5 minutes. Remove chee yee from heat and drain (reserve liquid). Heat wok and when hot add oil. When oil has heated almost to smoking point, about 1 minute, take wok off heat, add chee yee, place wok back on heat and stir-fry with snow peas, carrots, celery and water chestnuts for 2 minutes. Pour in stock (left from cooking chee yee), cover with a lid and simmer for 2 minutes. Blend cornflour with water and stir into vegetable mixture until thickened. Sprinkle with sesame soy to glisten and ladle into noodle basket. (See photograph p49.)

Cauliflower, Water Chestnuts and Champignons

Yeah Choy Farr, Mar Tay, Doong Gwoo

1 small cauliflower
2 cups water
1 tablespoon oil
1 clove garlic, crushed
1 piece fresh green ginger, crushed
1 small can champignons, drained
10 water chestnuts
¾ cup stock
salt and pepper
2 teaspoons cornflour
2 teaspoons water
2 teaspoons soy sauce
1 teaspoon sesame oil

Cut the cauliflower into flowerets and rinse. Blanch for 1 minute in 2 cups of boiling water. Remove and drain. Heat wok and when hot add oil, garlic and ginger. Stir-fry cauliflower, champignons and water chestnuts for 1 minute. Pour in stock, season with salt and pepper, cover with a lid and simmer for 1 minute. Blend cornflour with water then pour into vegetables and stir until sauce thickens. Add soy sauce and sesame oil just before serving.

*If using fresh mushrooms, do not overcook.

Pumpkin in Black Bean Sauce

Narm Gwah Dow See Jup

1 kg (2 lbs) ironbark pumpkin
2 tablespoons black beans (dow see)
½ teaspoon sesame oil
1 teaspoon sugar
2 tablespoons brandy
1 tablespoon vegetable oil
2 cups water
1 tablespoon chopped parsley

Cut skin off pumpkin and remove seeds. Cut into 5 cm (2 in) lengths. Wash black beans and place in a bowl. Mash, then mix with sesame oil, sugar and brandy. Heat wok and when hot add oil and stir-fry pumpkin, do not allow to burn. Then pour in water, cook pumpkin until tender then mix in black beans. Cover with a lid, add a little more water if necessary, and simmer for 5 minutes. The pumpkin should have absorbed all the moisture, be tender and still in one piece. Serve sprinkled with chopped parsley. See photograph p8.

Braised Mushrooms and Bamboo Shoots with Gingko Nuts

Doong Gwoo, Jook Sun Chow Bark Gwor

60 g (2 oz) Chinese mushrooms, soaked in water for 20 minutes
1 litre vegetable stock
250 g (8 oz) fresh bamboo shoots
1 small can gingko nuts
2 tablespoons vegetable oil
1 tablespoon oyster sauce
1 teaspoon soy sauce
1 tablespoon cornflour
2 tablespoons water
1 teaspoon sesame-soy

Rinse mushrooms and put in large saucepan with stock. Bring to the boil then simmer for 10 minutes. Remove mushrooms and discard stalks. Keep stock. Slice bamboo shoots very thinly. Drain liquid from gingko nuts. Heat wok and when hot add oil until smoking. Remove wok from heat and put in mushrooms, return to heat and stir-fry for 1 minute, then add bamboo shoots and gingko nuts to heat through. Pour in 1 cup of vegetable stock, cover with a lid and simmer for 2 minutes. Mix in oyster sauce and soy sauce and stir in cornflour blended with water until sauce thickens. Just before serving, mix in sesame-soy to glisten. Decorate with a chilli flower and cucumber garnish. See photograph below.

*If gingko nuts are fresh, crack shells with a small hammer and remove the nut. Boil in water to cover and cook for 20 minutes or until the brown skin is removed easily.

Cucumber and Onion Salad

Leung Gwah

1 cucumber
½ cup lemon juice
2 tablespoons water
1 tablespoon vegetable oil
2 cloves garlic, finely sliced
1 large onion, finely sliced
½ teaspoon tumeric
1 teaspoon raw sugar
1 tomato

Peel cucumber and remove seeds. Cut into slices and heat in wok with 2 tablespoons lemon juice and water for 1 minute. Remove to salad bowl. Dry wok and heat oil and garlic together. Stir-fry onions until golden brown. Remove to platter and allow to cool. Add tumeric, raw sugar, 1 tablespoon lemon juice to heat together in wok, then mix into cucumber. Sprinkle onions on top. Decorate with tomato wedges. See photograph p69.

Jade Salad

Yook Choy Salat

1 bunch white cabbage (bark choy), green leaves only
1 bunch flowering chives
1 stem coriander

Dressing
1 clove garlic, finely chopped
½ teaspoon salt
½ teaspoon mustard powder
½ cup lemon juice
1 teaspoon sugar
1 cup vegetable oil
¼ cup sesame-soy

Wash white cabbage leaves and soak in cool water for 30 minutes, when they will bloom out and crisp. Drain and dry on absorbent paper. Roll leaves within each other and shred. Hold bunch of flowering chives still strung together and cut off hard stem ends. Wash whilst still strung together. Cut into 4 cm (1 ½ in) lengths. The flowering buds are edible. Drain and dry on absorbent paper. Wash coriander and remove root and stems (keep for vegetable stock pot). Separate green leaves from stem. Dry on absorbent paper. Place all the greens in a serving dish and mix in dressing. Decorate with a carved carrot rose. See photograph p53.

To make dressing: place chopped garlic in a small bowl and sprinkle on salt and mustard. Pour in lemon juice and add sugar. Stir in vegetable oil and sesame-soy. Mix thoroughly before pouring over vegetable greens.

Taro Root Baskets

See Jay Larm

1 kg (2 lbs) taro root or potatoes
1 teaspoon cornflour
½ teaspoon salt
oil for deep-frying

Peel taro root or potatoes and cut into shreds. Sprinkle with cornflour and salt. Place shreds in a ladle and place a smaller ladle on top to press together. Heat oil in deep pan and cooked shredded taro root until golden brown. Drain on absorbent paper. The baskets are filled with a variety of fillings. Depending on size of baskets, the yield will be 2 or 3 baskets. These can be cooked beforehand and carefully kept in an airtight tin.

Suggested fillings: sliced prawns, vegetables, chicken or seafood.

Noodle Basket

Mein Larm

500 g (1 lb) flat spaghetti noodles
6 cups vegetable oil

Cook spaghetti noodles in boiling water for 10 minutes. Refresh with cold water and drain lightly.

Take 6 strands of noodles and fold over index finger. Put in deep perforated strainer with no handle (colander type). Drape loop over edge. Intertwine ends in colander to ensure they will not move when cooking. Place more noodles in the centre. Place colander on top to make basket shape.

Heat oil in wok and when hot immerse colander and deep-fry noodles until golden brown. Drain on absorbent paper.

See photograph p49, also photograph p56, using cellophane noodles as basket.

Braised Mushrooms, Bamboo Shoots and Gingko Nuts (p32), My Favourite Chicken Curry (p54), Green Apple Swans (p39), grapefruit salad and Shallot Pancakes (p38).

Stir-Fry Vegetables

2-3 stalks Chinese vegetable – choy sum, gai larn, bark choy, oong choy
2 tablespoons vegetable oil
1 clove garlic, crushed
1 piece fresh green ginger, shredded
1 teaspoon soy sauce
V1 teaspoon oyster sauce
1 teaspoon barbecue sauce (hoi sin)
2 tablespoons stock
2 tablespoons rose wine or sherry
1 teaspoon sesame-soy
water chestnuts and carrots for garnish

Separate stalks from green leaves. Peel any hard fibres from stalk of vegetable with a vegetable peeler, wash thoroughly and cut into 4 cm (1 ¼ in) lengths. Heat wok and when hot add oil, garlic and shredded ginger. When smoking, remove browned garlic. Take wok from heat, put in stalks, return to heat and stir-fry for 1 minute. Add washed green leaves, and mix together. Mix in soy sauce, oyster sauce, barbecue sauce and add stock. Cook together for another minute or until stalks are tender. Sprinkle with rose wine. Just before serving, add sesame-soy. Decorate with water chestnuts and 'butterfly' carrots. See photograph opposite.

*If no sesame-soy, which is a mild blend of the two oils, use ½ teaspoon sesame oil.

Cutting carrots to make ornamental shapes to garnish stir-fry vegetables.

Preparing water spinach (oong choy) – taking leaves off the vines.

Fresh Mustard Cabbage Soup (p44); Rice Noodles (p37) and Bean Sprout Noodles (p39) and Stir-fry Vegetables (above).

Bean Sprout Salad

Knar Choy

500 g (1 lb) fresh bean sprouts
1 lemon
½ teaspoon salt
1 tablespoon vegetable oil, warm
½ cup Chinese vinaigrette sauce (see p78)
lettuce leaves, washed and crisped in refrigerator (place washed lettuce in water and leave in cool part of refrigerator for 1 hour)
1 cup diced papaya
2 tablespoons maiden hair seaweed (fatt choy)

Remove tips and root ends from bean sprouts and wash thoroughly. Drain. Place bean sprouts in salad bowl, squeeze in lemon juice, add salt and mix in warm vegetable oil. Pour in Chinese vinaigrette and toss vegetables. Drain and dry lettuce leaves. Break into pieces and mix with bean sprouts. Serve topped with diced papaya and maiden hair seaweed.

*Wash maiden hair thoroughly and soak in warm water for 10 minutes. Boil for 15 minutes in 1 cup of seasoned stock. Remove, and cut into short lengths.

White Turnip Salad

Lo Bark

1 white turnip
salt
250 g (8 oz) soy bean sprouts, blanched
½ bunch watercress
¼ cup Chinese vinaigrette sauce (see p77)
½ bunch radishes

Dressing for turnips
½ cup lemon juice
2 tablespoons sugar
½ teaspoon sesame oil

Peel white turnip and cut into julienne shapes. Mix in salt, squeeze dry and then place in bowl of water to refresh. Chill in refrigerator for 1 hour. Rinse soy bean sprouts then drain thoroughly. Wash watercress and break into small sprays. Drain turnips thoroughly then toss in dressing. Place in serving dish. Put soy beans on top then top with sliced radishes and watercress. Pour over the vinaigrette dressing and serve immediately. See photograph p66.

Home-made Pickles

Garteng Sin Choy

2 white turnips (lo bark), cut into wedges
3-4 carrots, cut into rounds
250 g (8 oz) cauliflower, separate flowerettes, cut stems
20 radishes
2 onions, cut into wedges
20 green beans
16 cups water
1 whole piece fresh green ginger, skin removed
4 hot red chillies
½ cup salt
½ cup rice wine

Thoroughly wash and dry vegetables. Cut large vegetables in smaller lengths or wedges. Boil water and add all the seasonings. Allow to cool. Place all the vegetables, the harder types at the bottom, in a glass jar. Pour in the seasoning mixture. Cover with a greaseproof paper lid. Tie securely. Vegetables should be ready in 2-3 days time. Use dry, clean chopsticks when removing vegetables from brine. Use any vegetables in season.

Brown Rice with Mushrooms

2 tablespoons vegetable oil
3 cups cooked brown rice, cold
½ cup cooked shrimps or dried shrimps (har mei)
60g (2oz) fresh mushrooms, diced
1 piece fresh bamboo shoot, diced
1 cooked carrot, diced
½ cup vegetable stock
1 tablespoon soy sauce
few lengths of shallots, diced
bean sprouts for garnish

Heat wok, add oil and when hot add brown rice. Stir-fry for 1 minute. Add shrimps, mushrooms, bamboo shoots and carrot and stir-fry continuously. Pour in stock and soy sauce and mix in shallots. Cover with a lid and allow to heat through for 5 minutes. Serve hot, sprinkled with a few bean sprouts.

Rice Noodles

Chow Sar Hor Fun

250 g (8 oz) fresh rice noodles
1 tablespoon sesame oil
125 g (4 oz) bean sprouts
¼ cup vegetable oil
1 small onion, finely sliced
2 tablespoons soy sauce
2 stalks shallots, cut in slivers
ground pepper to taste

Slice rice noodles into ribbons 1 cm (¼ in) wide, and as these are already cooked when purchased just drop in boiling water for 10 minutes, then drain. Sprinkle with sesame oil. Remove roots from bean sprouts, wash and drain. (Leave in water until ready for use.) Heat wok and when hot add oil. Put in onion and stir-fry for ½ minute. Then put in rice noodles and mix together, but do not allow noodles to brown. Sprinkle with soy sauce and keep on stir-frying until sauce colours the rice noodles. Mix in shallots and serve with a sprinkling of ground pepper. See photograph below.

Rice noodles and bean sprout noodles.

Flattening dough into circles for Shallot Pancakes.

Sprinkling pancakes with shallots then rolling up longways and flattening again.

Standing dough up (right), then flattening into a round shape again.

Frying both sides of pancake until golden brown.

Shallot Pancakes

Choong Beang

1 cup flour
½ cup boiling water
oil for brushing
½ cup shallots or chives, chopped
½ teaspoon salt
1 tablespoon oil

Sift flour in a bowl and add boiling water gradually, mixing with bamboo chopsticks (or wooden spoon). Add a little cold water if dough appears too dry. Knead into a smooth dough. Roll into a long roll and cut in 6-8 pieces. Flatten each section into a 10 cm (4 in) circle. Brush on a little oil, sprinkle with shallots and salt. Roll up and flatten with rolling pin. Roll to make a long shape. Stand dough up with rolled surface facing downwards. Roll out to flatten into a 10 cm (4 in) circle again. Allow to stand for 10 minutes. Heat oil in wok and when moderately hot, fry on both sides until golden brown. Serve with main course, and garnish with a green apple swan - see recipe and photograph opposite.

*Speciality of Kenny Lau, Imperial Peking Restaurants.

Egg Roll

Gai Darn Guern

6 eggs
¼ cup vegetable oil

Filling
500 g (1 lb) made up of the following, cut into matchstick pieces –
carrot
onion
bean sprouts
bamboo shoots
cabbage
fresh mushrooms
1 teaspoon soy sauce
¼ teaspoon five-spice powder
ground pepper

oil for deep-frying

Beat eggs together making sure that they are well-belended and then strain through a muslin cloth so there is a smooth mixture. Heat the wok, add 1 tablespoon of oil and rotate it around the wok to lubricate a little more than halfway up the sides of wok. Pour off any excess. When moderately hot, ladle in one quarter of the egg mixture and rotate it to make a thin large skin, about 20cm (8in) in diameter. If the wok is oiled correctly it will fall out of the pan without sticking. Place on upturned plate to cool. Makes 4 egg rolls.

Heat wok and stir-fry your selection of vegetables till limp. Season with soy sauce, five-spice powder and ground pepper. Allow to cool.

Divide mixture into 4 portions and roll in egg skin, tucking in the edges securely – if necessary, brush edges with a little beaten egg or water. Chill in refrigerator for 1 hour or longer to enable egg roll to firm. When ready to serve, deep-fry until lightly brown. Drain on absorbent paper. Serve egg roll by slicing into oblique slices.

Bean Sprout Noodles

Knar Choy Mein

1 Chinese rice bowl of fresh bean sprouts
2 tablespoons vegetable oil
3 stems shallots
few slivers fresh green ginger
85 g (3 oz) pkt instant noodles
1 tablespoon sesame oil
1 teaspoon soy sauce
1 tablespoon water
1 tablespoon of satay or oyster sauce
salt and pepper

Wash bean sprouts, remove any discoloured tips or roots, and soak in cool water. Drain. Slice shallots into oblique 2 cm (1 in) lengths. Heat wok and when hot add 1 tablespoon oil and stir-fry bean sprouts, shallots and ginger for 1 minute. Remove to serving platter. Boil noodles according to directions on packet. Remove from heat and pour off water. Rinse well with cool water and drain. Mix in sesame oil. Heat wok and when hot add 1 tablespoon vegetable oil and stir-fry noodles. Add soy sauce, water, satay sauce, bean sprout mixture and seasoning. Continue to stir-fry all the time so as not to allow noodles to stick to wok. Serve with mango pickles and chilli sauce. See photographs pp8 and 34.

Gow Choy Omelette

4-5 eggs
½ bunch chives (gow choy), to make up 1 cup
2 tablespoons vegetable stock or water
¼ teaspoon sesame oil
¼ teaspoon soy sauce
¼ cup corn oil

Beat eggs together in a bowl. Wash and drain chives. Dry with absorbent paper. Cut into 2.5 cm (1 in) lengths. Stir vegetable stock, sesame oil and soy sauce into beaten eggs. Mix in chives. Heat oil and when hot spoon in one quarter of mixture and cook one side until golden brown and set. Then fold over to make a half moon shape. Cook a further ½ minute but do not overcook. Place on heated platter.

Cook remainder of mixture, placing omelettes on top of each other as they are cooked. Serve with steamed rice. Serves 4.

Green Apple 'Swan'

2 large granny smith apples
salt
2 lemons
cloves (match heads or cherries, can be used as 'eyes').

Choose unblemished bright green granny smith apples. Stand apple upright and slice off piece from side. Sprinkle with salt and brush cut side with lemon juice. This side will be the base, so leave cut side flat on working surface. Cut 2 wedges from each side of top part of apple leaving a 1-cm wide strip to form backbone. Carefully cut each wedge 7-8 times (depending on size of apple) into an 'L' which is moveable. Return wedge to 'body' and gently push out slices backwards to form wings and tail. Cut a curved neck from the other apple and shape top into 'head'. Insert 2 small cloves to make eyes. Fasten neck with a strong toothpick and secure at the core end of apple. Brush all gently with lemon juice. See photograph below.

Green Apple 'Swan'.

1.Peeling taro for Vegetarian Spring Rolls and Dim Sims.

2.Soaking taro in water and cutting into fine dice.

3.Two different methods of wrapping Spring Rolls.

Vegetarian Spring Rolls

Filling
taro root
carrot
mushrooms
celery
onion
cabbage
bamboo shoots
1 tablespoon vegetable oil
salt and pepper
1 teaspoon bean paste (min see jeung)

10 spring roll wrappers
2 cups vegetable oil

Boil taro root until tender, then mash. Allow to cool. Taro root is the base, so use a selection of the other vegetables all cut into matchstick pieces. Heat wok and when hot add oil. When smoking, stir-fry the matchstick pieces of vegetables until limp. Season with salt and pepper and bean paste. Allow to cool.

Mix with mashed taro root and divide into 10 portions shaped in a log shape. Roll in spring roll wrappers, seal edges with water or milk and wrap into a secure roll. Place in a cool place in refrigerator for 1-2 hours to set the filling. Deep-fry in hot oil until golden brown. Drain on absorbent paper. Decorate with flowering chives and carrot garnish. See photograph opposite.

*Spring roll skins can be purchased in oriental supermarkets, or make up your own pastry or use filo pastry.

Vegetarian Dim Sims

Filling
taro root
carrot
mushrooms
celery
onion
cabbage
bamboo shoots
a tablespoon vegetable oil
salt and pepper
1 teaspoon bean paste (min see jeung)

15 pieces dim sim pastry
1 teaspoon cornflour
2 cups vegetable oil

Boil taro root until tender, then mash. Allow to cool. Taro root is the base, so use a selection of the other vegetables all cut into matchstick pieces. Heat wok and when hot add oil. When smoking, stir-fry the matchstick pieces of vegetables until limp. Season with salt and pepper and bean paste. Allow to cool.

Mix with the mashed taro root and divide into 15 portions, shaped into round balls. Place inside dim sim pastry and close up loosely all round filling. Dip open end into a little cornflour. Deep-fry in hot oil until golden brown. Drain on absorbent paper. Serve with a clear sweet-sour sauce. See photograph right.

Making rabbits for decoration out of apples and cucumber.

Vegetarian Dim Sims (p40), Vegetarian Spring Rolls (p40) and fruit with rabbit decorations.

Vegetable Soups

Lotus Soup

Lin Kno Tong

½ bunch mustard cabbage (gai choy)
2 cakes deep-fried beancurd
6 cups stock
1 stock cube
1 can lotus root
2 sweet potatoes, cooked
salt and pepper

Cut 1 cm off bottom stem of mustard cabbage. Separate stalks from green leaves and cut into 5 cm (2 in) pieces. Wash thoroughly. Cut beancurd into very small dice. Heat stock in a large saucepan and sprinkle in stock cube. Keep simmering and put in hard stems to cook for 1 minute then add cubed sweet potatoes, green leaves and lotus root. Cook until mustard cabbage is tender, then remove and place in soup tureen. Allow lotus root to cook for a further 10 minutes and adjust seasoning. Ladle hot soup and lotus root over vegetables. Sprinkle with diced beancurd. See photograph below.

Preparing vegetables for Lotus Soup (sweet potatoes, separated leaves and stalks of mustard cabbage and lotus root).

Lotus Soup.

Dried Chinese White Cabbage Soup

Bark Choy Gawn Tong

125 g (4 oz) dried Chinese white cabbage (bark choy gawn)
2 pork chops
soup vegetables (chopped onion, celery, parsley)
2 cakes fresh beancurd (tao fu) cut into 1.2 cm (½ in) cubes
salt and pepper

Wash dried Chinese white cabbage and soak for at least 1 hour. Drain and cut into 5 cm (2 in) lengths. Place in a large saucepan with water to cover and bring to the boil. Reduce heat and simmer for 1 ½-2 hours (reserve liquid).

Make stock by simmering pork chops and soup vegetables for 1½ hours. Remove pork when tender and when cool cut into dice. Place stock in refrigerator overnight, then remove fat from surface and strain.

Place in a clean saucepan together with the liquid from cooking of dried vegetable, bring to the boil and simmer for 15 minutes. Return pork meat and add beancurd. Correct seasoning and simmer for 5-10 minutes more. Serve hot.

Fresh Green Pea Egg-Flower Soup

Cheng Dow Darn Farr Tong

8 cups beef stock, seasoned (or use 2 stock cubes)
500 g (1 lb) fresh green peas, shelled
1 egg
coriander leaves

Bring beef stock to the boil. Add green peas and simmer for 8-10 minutes until tender. Beat egg lightly in a bowl and pour into hot soup, stirring constantly until egg separates into threads. Adjust seasoning. Serve immediately with garnish of coriander leaves.

Pork, Watercress and Loong Narn Soup

Jee Yuk Choy Tong

1 kg (2 lbs) lean pork
1 stick celery
1 carrot
1 onion
30 g (1 oz) dried dragon's eyes (loong narn)
1 bunch watercress
salt and pepper
½ teaspoon sesame oil

Boil pork until tender, in enough water to cover, with chopped celery, carrot and onion. Remove pork and allow soup to cool in refrigerator overnight, lift off any fat. Next day, cut pork into slices. Bring soup to the boil and add loong narn and sliced pork and simmer for 20 minutes. Wash watercress and separate stalks from green leaves Add stalks, simmer 5 minutes, then put in green leaves and simmer for another 5 minutes. Correct seasoning.

To serve, place watercress at bottom of soup tureen and pour on warm sesame oil. Then ladle in the hot soup with slices of pork and dragon's eyes.

*Dragon's eyes – also called dragon seeds – are a sweet, small, grape-like fruit of the lychee family.

Chinese Spinach Soup

Een Choy Tong

1 bunch Chinese spinach (een choy, green leaf variety)
6 cups seasoned stock (vegetable or chicken)
1 sweet potato (orange colour) diced and cooked until tender
½ teaspoon salt
1 tablespoon vegetable oil
1 teaspoon sesame oil

Prepare spinach as mentioned on p11. Heat stock in large wok or saucepan and bring to the boil. Add sweet potato. Put in spinach and simmer until limp, about 10 minutes. Add salt. Heat vegetable and sesame oils.

To serve, place the spinach in soup tureen and spoon over the hot oils. Ladle in the sweet potato and hot soup.

Carrot Soup

Hoong Loh Bark Tong

1 kg (2 lbs) carrots
1 onion
few stalks celery
1 bunch coriander
4 cups water
1 cup cooked rice
salt and pepper
2 cups cream
coriander leaves

Wash, peel and chop up vegetables and place in a large saucepan with water to cover. Bring to the boil and then simmer until vegetables are tender, replenishing water when required. Add rice, salt and pepper and simmer for a further 15 minutes. Strain off most of the liquid (retain) and blend vegetables and rice in a blender. Reheat stock with blended vegetables, correct seasoning. In the last 5 minutes of cooking, stir in cream. Serve hot with coriander leaves.

*Original recipe calls for glutinous rice which thickens the soup naturally.

White Turnip and Flank Soup

Bark Narm Lor Bark Tong

500 g (1 lb) flank steak
1 teaspoon vegetable oil
1 small onion, diced
½ teaspoon peppercorns
¼ dried mandarin skin
500 g (1 lb) white turnips
1 cup rose wine
salt
2 tablespoons chopped shallots
coriander leaves

Cut flank steak into chunks, do not remove gristle. Using a wok or deep saucepan, heat oil and brown the meat and onion. Cover with water and add peppercorns. Simmer for 30 minutes. Soak mandarin skin in water until soft and cut into fine strips. Wash and peel turnips and cut obliquely into large pieces. Put mandarin skin and turnips into the soup, replenish with water or rose wine, and continue simmering until meat and vegetables are tender. Add salt to taste. Serve sprinkled with shallots and coriander leaves.

*Gristle retains the gelatinous quality which adds flavour to the soup.

Head Cabbage Soup

Yeah Choy Tong

¼ of a wedge from a medium-sized head cabbage, about 250 g (8 oz)
1 tablespoon vegetable oil
1 clove garlic, crushed
2 cups seasoned vegetable stock
¼ teaspoon soy sauce
salt and pepper
¼ teaspoon sesame-soy

Cut cabbage up roughly into 4 cm (1 ½ in) pieces, wash thoroughly and drain. Heat wok and when hot add oil and garlic. Remove garlic when oil sizzles, take wok from flame and put in cabbage (this is so the sizzle is away from the flame and safe). Return wok to flame and stir-fry for 1-2 minutes. Pour in stock and soy sauce and allow to simmer until cabbage is tender. Adjust seasoning by adding salt and pepper. Ladle cabbage in soup tureen and pour over the hot soup. Sprinkle with sesame-soy on serving.

*Served as extra vegetable.

Fresh Mustard Cabbage Soup

Gai Choy Tong

1 bunch mustard cabbage
2 squares fresh beancurd (tao fu)
1 cup vegetable oil
8 cups hot seasoned stock
½ teaspoon soy sauce
½ teaspoon sesame soy

Wash mustard cabbage carefully and cut into 5 cm (2 in) lengths. Separate hard stems from green leaves. Dry fresh beancurd thoroughly with absorbent paper. Cut into small dice. Heat oil in wok and deep-fry beancurd until golden brown. Drain.

Heat seasoned stock then put in hard stems and cook for 3 minutes. Then add leaves and cook for another 2 minutes.

To serve, ladle vegetables in a soup tureen, sprinkle with soy sauce and sesame soy, ladle on hot soup and sprinkle with toasted beancurd. See photograph p34.

Winter Melon Soup

Doong Gwah Joong (a festive occasion soup)

2 chickens
1 large winter melon (doong gwah)
½ cup lotus nuts (lin jee)
10 Chinese mushrooms, soaked in warm water for 20 minutes then diced
10 red dates (hoong joh)
1 piece bamboo shoot, diced
250 g (8 oz) lean pork, diced
10 fresh prawns
½ cup crabmeat
1 can abalone, diced (reserve liquid)
1 tablespoon minced shallots
2 slices cooked ham

Retain chicken breasts and make concentrated stock with rest of chicken. Strain. Remove skin and bones from chicken breast and cut into small 1.5 cm (½ in) dice.

Wipe melon and cut off one-quarter from top to form a lid. Tie string around melon to form a string bag so it will be easy to lift. Set melon in a large pot so it fits securely. Set this pot in another larger pot with enough space between the two pots to fill with water to enable steaming. Fill melon two-thirds full with hot chicken stock and add lotus nuts, mushrooms, red dates and bamboo shoots. Replace top of melon (lid). Fill space between pots with boiling water and replenish when water gets low. Steam for 2-3 hours or until melon meat becomes soft and transparent.

Place diced chicken breast, pork and stock in another saucepan and bring to the boil. Simmer for 5 minutes. Five minutes before serving, add prawns, crab and diced abalone and liquid to heat through. Correct seasoning.

Lift melon out carefully by the strings and lower it into a deep bowl where it can stand upright. Ladle in the contents of the other saucepan and some of the soup. Sprinkle top with finely chopped shallots and ham.

To serve, spoon out the melon meat with soup and filling in each individual bowl. See photograph below.

*Choose a large mature melon that has a tough skin and can stand the long process of steaming. Make sure that it will fit into your largest pot.
*If you want to present a carved winter melon, it cannot be steamed as it will change in colour, become too soft and the carving will be spoiled. I suggest you place your carved melon on a shallow dish and ladle in the cooked soup, keeping the balance in a soup tureen for serving.

Winter Melon Soup.

Vegetables with Seafood

Snow Pea Tendrils with Crab Sauce

Hollan Doe Yip

1 kg (2 lbs) snow pea tendrils
3 tablespoons vegetable oil
1 piece fresh green ginger, slivered
¼ cup rose wine

Crab Sauce
1 ½ cups vegetable stock
½ teaspoon salt
1 tablespoon cornflour
1 tablespoon water
125 g (4 oz) crabmeat, cooked
1 egg white
1 teaspoon sesame-soy

2 tablespoons toasted cellophane noodles

Wash snow pea tendrils thoroughly and drain. Cut into shorter lengths with scissors. Heat wok and when hot add oil and ginger. As ginger browns, discard, and put in snow pea tendrils. Stir-fry until vegetable limps, about 1 minute, then pour in rose wine and cook a further ½ minute. Ladle on to serving platter and spoon over crab sauce.

To make crab sauce: Boil stock and salt together for 5 minutes and then turn down to simmer. Blend cornflour with water, and stir into stock until thickened. Put in crabmeat to heat through and stir in egg white. Just before serving sprinkle with sesame-soy. Pour over the snow pea tendrils. Garnish with toasted cellophane noodles.

Skewered Crab Balls

Hai Yin

500 g (1 lb) cooked crabmeat
1 cup soft breadcrumbs
1 tablespoon chopped shallots
1 tablespoon chopped coriander stalks
salt and pepper
500 g (1 lb) streaky bacon

Place crabmeat in a bowl and mix in the breadcrumbs. Sprinkle on the shallots and coriander stalks and work into crab mixture. Correct seasonings. Roll into small balls the size of walnuts. Wrap with bacon and skewer securely with strong toothpicks. Thread 3 on a wooden skewer and cook under griller until bacon is cooked, turning occasionally.

*When using bamboo skewers, soak in water first. Cover exposed end of skewer with aluminium foil so as skewer will not burn during cooking process.

Chives with Seafood Sticks

Gow Gee Har

1 bunch chives
2 cooked carrots
6 seafood sticks
½ cup vegetable oil
1 cup soy bean sprouts
2 tablespoons vegetable stock
salt and pepper

Rinse bunch of chives – keeping them strung together. Cut off ends and then cut into 5 cm (2 in) lengths. Cut cooked carrot into same size. Slice seafood sticks obliquely into approximately the same size lengths.

Heat wok, and when hot add oil. When moderately hot, stir-fry carrot and soy bean sprouts for 1 minute, add chives and stock and mix together until chives are slightly limp. Add seafood sticks and mix until heated through. Adjust seasoning.

Cutting technique for summer melon. Other Chinese vegetables in photograph are, from back to front, mustard cabbage, Tiensin cabbage, Chinese spinach and Chinese flowering vegetable.

Summer Melon with Crab Omelette (above) and Meat roll on Cellophane Noodles (p62).

Summer Melon with Crab Omelette

Jit Gwah Hi Darn

1 small summer melon (jit gwah), approx. 2 kg (4 lb)
125 g (4 oz) cellophane noodles (jun see)
few shallots
3 eggs
1 teaspoon water
1 small can crabmeat (or fresh crabmeat is best)
6 tablespoons vegetable oil
1 piece fresh green ginger, shredded
1 cup vegetable stock

Peel summer melon, remove seeds and cut the flesh into matchstick pieces. Place in a bowl of cold water and prepare other ingredients. Soak cellophane noodles in cold water for 10 minutes and use scissors to cut into 10 cm (4 in) lengths. Drain. Cut shallots into matchstick pieces. Separate the crab into strands. Beat egg together with water and add half the crabmeat.

Heat wok and when hot add 1 tablespoon oil. Pour in one-third of egg mixture and make a round omelette, gently browned on both sides. Make 2 more omelettes with balance of egg mixture. Set aside on warming platter. Add 3 more tablespoons of oil to wok and heat. Put in ginger and summer melon, turn over once with spatula, then pour in stock. Add cellophane noodles, balance of crabmeat, shallots and mix well together. Serve with crab omelette on top. See photograph below.

Separating leaves and stalks of Chinese white cabbage. Other ingredients: chopped carrot, seafood sticks and chives.

Dicing fresh and pickled mustard cabbage.

Chrysanthemum vegetable and barbecued pork.

Chinese White Cabbage with Seafood Sticks

Bark Choy

1 bunch Chinese white cabbage (bark choy)
2 carrots
1 red capsicum
½ bunch flowering chives
6 seafood sticks
2 tablespoons vegetable oil
1 piece fresh green ginger, sliced
½ cup water or vegetable stock
1 teaspoon soy sauce
1 teaspoon sesame oil

Prepare Chinese white cabbage as directed on p9 and cut white stalks only into strips (see step-by-step photo left). Use green leaves for salad or mermaid tresses. Cut carrot, capsicum, flowering chives into same shape. Cut seafood sticks into halves then same size lengths as the vegetables. Heat wok and when hot add oil and ginger. Put in Chinese white cabbage stalks and stir-fry for ½ minute. Add carrot, water and soy sauce and mix together. Allow to cook for a further minute then add capsicum and chives. Stir-fry until Chinese white cabbage is tender, about another minute. Then add seafood sticks and heat through. The dish should not be too moist because it is being presented in a noodle basket (see p33). If you wish to serve it on a platter, increase the water to 1 cup and blend in 1 tablespoon cornflour to thicken the sauce. Spoon over sesame oil to glisten. See photograph opposite.

Vegetarian Prawn Curry

Gar Lee Har

1 large, fresh, unripe coconut
yellow colouring
2 tablespoons oil
1 onion, diced
2 cloves garlic, chopped
2 tablespoons curry powder
2 potatoes, cooked and diced
4 cups water
1 teaspoon salt
2 hot chillies, finely sliced
2 tablespoons cornflour
3 tablespoons water

Remove fibres and crack shell to remove coconut meat. Scrape off brown skin and rinse under cool water. Cut coconut meat into small 'prawn' shapes and place in bowl of cool water. Put in yellow colouring and allow to stand for 1 hour. Drain.

Heat wok, add oil and when hot stir-fry onion and garlic for 1 minute. Sprinkle in curry powder, stir until fragrant then add potatoes and water. Bring to the boil, then reduce heat. Add coconut 'prawns' and simmer for 15 minutes. Season with salt and add hot chillies to heat through. Blend cornflour with water and cook into mixture until thickened. Serve with steamed rice.

*The soft flesh of coconut when coloured is an excellent substitute for prawns in vegetarian dishes.

Chinese White Cabbage with Seafood Sticks (above) and Mixed Vegetables with Oyster Sauce (p31) in Noodle Baskets (p33), garnished with Mermaid Tresses (p26); Pickled Mustard Cabbage (p27) garnished with a tomato rose, and Chrysanthemum Vegetable with Barbecue Pork (p67).

Curried Prawn and Rice

Gar Lee Har

4 tablespoons vegetable oil
1 teaspoon sesame oil
1 piece fresh green ginger, crushed
250 g (8 oz) raw shelled prawns
2 cloves garlic, crushed
1 onion, sliced top to bottom
2 tablespoons curry powder
3 large potatoes, diced
2 bay leaves
2 large tomatoes
4 cups water
1 stock cube, crushed
¼ teaspoon soy sauce
¼ teaspoon salt
¼ cup cream
parsley or coriander
steamed hot rice

Heat wok and when hot add 2 tablespoons vegetable oil and sesame oil. Put in green ginger and when it sizzles, stir-fry the prawns until coloured. Retain liquid. Remove to platter.

Heat wok again, add 2 tablespoons vegetable oil and crushed garlic. Allow to sizzle then stir in onions to limp. Sprinkle in curry powder and stir all the time so as nothing sticks at the bottom of wok. Put in diced potatoes, bay leaves, tomatoes, stock cube, water to cover and bring to the boil. Lower heat and simmer with a lid until potatoes are tender. Stir occasionally. Put in soy sauce and salt. Remove bay leaves and strain curry sauce through a coarse sieve.

Heat sauce again, add a little water if too thick, and put in prawns and liquid from prawns to heat through. Just before serving, stir in cream to enrich. Sprinkle with chopped coriander or parsley and serve with steamed hot rice.

*Coconut cream may be substituted.

Avocado Shrimp Balls

Gor Lee Har Yin

3 firm, ripe avocadoes
500 g (1 lb) cooked shrimps

Dressing
juice of 2 lemons to make up ¼ cup lemon juice
1 cup salad oil
½ teaspoon salt
¼ teaspoon ground black pepper
1 teaspoon raw sugar
1 tablespoon chopped parsley
1 tablespoon chopped celery
1 tablespoon chopped shallots
1 teaspoon chilli sauce

Ball out avocadoes with a melon baller and place balls on the bottom of 6 individual dishes. Divide the shrimps into 6 portions and place on top of avocado balls. Mix dressing ingredients together, correct seasoning and pour over avocado shrimps. Chill in refrigerator before serving.

*Keep a shrimp aside to place on side of dish for garnish.

Fresh Scallops with Black Bean Sauce

Dow See Dai Jee

10 fresh scallops (preferably with shells)
½ cup rose wine
chopped onion, celery leaves, coriander leaves, fresh thyme or basil
2 cups water

Black Bean Sauce
1 tablespoon dried black beans
1 teaspoon fresh green ginger minced
1 tablespoon sesame-soy
1 tablespoon rose wine or brandy
coriander leaves

Poach scallops for a few minutes in rose wine and chopped vegetables, then place in cool water for 5 minutes. Remove and drain.

Wash black beans thoroughly and place in a small basin. Mash with blunt end of a cleaver. Put in minced ginger, sesame-soy and rose wine or brandy. Put each scallop on a shell and spoon over ¼ teaspoon of black bean sauce. Place on plate and steam for 5 minutes. Garnish with coriander leaves and serve with fried brown rice.

Combination of vegetables and Inside-out Fish with Sweet-Sour Sauce (p52).

Cutting fish almost into 2 halves.

Removing the bones.

Scoring the fish.

Deep-frying, using a ladle.

Inside-Out Fish with Sweet-Sour Sauce

Jow Sin Tim Yue

750 g (1 ½ lbs) whole bream or schnapper
1 tablespoon cornflour
2 cups vegetable oil for deep-frying

Place scaled and cleaned fish, with head attached, on working board. Split the body in half through to head. Remove backbone and cut off side fins with scissors. Score the fish, through flesh side, (underside), diagonally in a criss-cross patttern, nearly through to skin. Sprinkle with cornflour. See step-by-step photographs, left.

Heat oil in wok and, holding fish by head, ladle on hot oil for 5 minutes then slide in whole fish to cook head portion. Remove and drain on absorbent paper. Place on warm serving platter. Spoon over sweet-sour sauce (see recipe p78). See photograph p51.

*'To score' is the cookery term meaning to cut a line. This is to facilitate cooking and in the case of the fish recipe above, makes a very decorative pattern.

Shrimps in Black Bean Sauce

Dow See Har

1 kg (2 lbs) fresh shrimps
2 tablespoons black beans(dow see)
¼ cup brandy
2 tablespoons vegetable oil
1 tablespoon fresh green ginger, shredded
1 teaspoon sesame oil
Chinese parsley

Shell shrimps, retaining head and tail. Remove intestinal tract and wash thoroughly, especially the head portion. Place on a deep plate ready for steaming. Rinse black beans with cool water, drain, and place in a small basin. Mash the beans, pour in brandy and vegetable oil and mix in the shredded ginger. Spoon over the shrimps and steam for 20 minutes. In the last minute of cooking add the sesame oil. Garnish with Chinese parsley. Delicious either hot or cold.

Yin and Yang Fish

2 bream
salt
1 tablespoon fresh green ginger, shredded
1 tablespoon whole soy bean paste
½ cup hot fish stock
12 shelled fresh prawns
¼ cup vegetable oil
½ teaspoon sesame oil
1 teaspoon soy sauce
garnish of shallot slivers

Wash and clean both bream and score on thickened part. Sprinkle inside and outside with salt. Have deep flat plate ready for steaming. Sprinkle plate with shredded ginger and place both fish, side by side, on top. Mix together soy bean paste and hot stock in a small bowl, then pour over both fish. Place prawns down centre in decorative pattern. Steam for 15 minutes. Heat vegetable and sesame oils together.

To serve, spoon soy sauce over both fish. Sprinkle with slivers of shallots and sizzle over the hot oils.

Vegetables with Poultry

Meatballs on Pastry (p61), Jade Salad (p33) and Tiensin Cabbage with Chicken P54), garnished with a white turnip bird (see step-by-step photographs, p54).

WHITE TURNIP BIRD

To make white turnip bird for garnish: slice turnip obliquely to make 2 wings.

Carve body and neck of bird out of remainder of turnip. Shape feathers with a sharp knife. Use red chilli for beak and black peppercorns for eyes. Sit bird on a piece of fresh green for balance.

My Favourite Chicken Curry.

Tiensin Cabbage with Chicken

Wong Ah Bark Gai

2 chicken breasts
¼ bunch tiensin cabbage (wong ah bark)
1 red or green capsicum
2 tablespoons vegetable oil
½ cup vegetable stock
salt and pepper
1 tablespoon cornflour
2 tablespoons water
1 tablespoon soy sauce

Remove skin and bone from chicken breasts and cut meat into 2 cm (¾ in) dice. Wash celery cabbage and cut into 4 cm (1½ in) slices. Cut capsicum into dice. Heat wok and when hot add oil and when smoking stir-fry chicken until it turns golden. Remove to serving platter. Stir-fry capsicum until limp. Remove to serving platter. Put stock in wok and heat. Add celery cabbage and cook for 3 minutes. There should be very little liquid left. Return capsicum and chicken to mix through. Season with salt and pepper. Blend cornflour with water and soy sauce. Cook into mixture until sauce thickens. Serve hot. See photograph p53.

*A bunch of celery cabbage is usually very large, enabling 2 or 3 dishes from the one vegetable.

My Favourite Chicken Curry

Garlee Gai

1 kg (2 lbs) whole chicken
1 tablespoon cornflour
1 piece fresh green ginger
1 large sweet potato
¼ cup vegetable oil
2-4 cloves garlic, crushed
1 onion, sliced
2 tablespoons curry powder (or mixture of your favourite blends)
2 teaspoons sesame-soy
2 bay leaves
1 tablespoon soy sauce
4 cups water
1 cup coconut cream

Prepare chicken by washing and removing blood clots inside carcass Dry thoroughly and cut off wings and legs – chop into 2-3 pieces. Separate back from breast by cutting through, then cut back and breast into halves, then chop through into 16 pieces. (Should have 24 pieces altogether.) Sprinkle with cornflour. Scrape skin from ginger and cut into thin slices. Dice potato. Heat wok and when hot, add 1 tablespoon oil, and stir-fry chicken and ginger until slightly coloured.

Heat large saucepan and put in balance of oil (2 tablespoons) and add garlic and sliced onion. Stir-fry until onion is limp, then put in curry powder and sesame-soy. Keep stirring to release fragrance of curry ingredients, then add potato, bay leaves, chicken and soy sauce. Pour in water, reduce heat and simmer until chicken is tender, reducing sauce to half. In the last 5 minutes of cooking stir in coconut cream. Garnish with sprig of coriander. Serve with brown rice. See photograph, left.

Transparent Noodles with Chicken

Jun See Gai

60 g (2 oz) transparent noodles (jun see)
1 cup vegetable oil
500 g (1 lb) chicken meat
salt
1 egg white
3 tablespoons cornflour
2 stalks celery, finely diced
1 onion, finely diced
2 tablespoons green peas, cooked
1 tablespoon vegetable stock
¼ cup rose wine or sherry
Chinese parsley

Cut transparent noodles with scissors into short lengths. Heat oil and deep-fry noodles – they will immediately rise to the top in a white mass if the temperature is correct. Test with a small strand. Do not allow to brown. Remove and drain on absorbent paper. Keep in an air-tight container to retain crispness.

Mince chicken meat finely and add salt, then mix in egg white and cornflour. Pour most of the oil from wok and heat again. Stir-fry chicken until it turns colour, then put in celery, onion and green peas and mix thoroughly. Add the stock and rose wine, cover with a lid and simmer for 1 minute. Remove lid and mix in half of the tansparent noodles to just limp. Put the balance of transparent noodles on serving platter and ladle chicken mixture on top. Garnish with Chinese parsley and serve immediately.

Bean Sprouts with Chicken Shreds

Knar Choy Gai See

2 chicken breasts
1 egg white
½ teaspoon salt
1 tablespoon rice wine
1 teaspoon cornflour
250 g (8 oz) bean sprouts
2 tablespoons vegetable oil
½ teaspoon sugar
salt and pepper
½ teaspoon sesame oil
1 teaspoon bean paste (min see jeung)
1 tablespoon water
1 tablespoon stock
1 tablespoon cornflour

Remove skins and bone from chicken breasts. Slice meat into shreds, similar to size of bean sprouts, and place in a bowl. Mix in egg white and salt, pour over rice wine and allow to marinate for 15 minutes. Mix in cornflour. Wash bean sprouts and remove any discoloured ends. Place in water until ready to cook. Heat wok, and when hot add oil and stir-fry chicken, a little at a time, until lightly coloured – do not burn. Remove to serving plate. Heat wok again, drain bean sprouts, and stir-fry for ½ minute. Add sugar, salt and pepper, sesame oil and bean paste and stock. Blend in cornflour with water and stir until thickened. Return chicken and mix thoroughly. Serve hot.

Pineapple Duck

Bor Lor Arp

1 fresh fat duck 2-2.5 kg (4-5 lbs)
3 cups vegetable oil
6 slices canned pineapple
½ cup pineapple juice
1 piece fresh green ginger, crushed
1 tablespoon cornflour
1 tablespoon water
1 tablespoon soy sauce
1 teaspoon sesame-soy

Clean duck and place in large saucepan of boiling water. Return to the boil, then simmer for 30 minutes. Allow to remain in saucepan for another 30 minutes. Remove duck and dry thoroughly. (Retain liquid.)

Heat oil in wok and baste duck with ladle until brown. Pour off the oil in wok and place in duck, together with pineapple pieces, pineapple juice, crushed ginger and 1 cup of water (from cooking of duck). Cover with a lid, and simmer for 20 minutes or until duck is tender. (If preferred, cook duck in the same manner in a deep saucepan.) Remove duck to warm serving platter.

Blend cornflour with water and stir into liquid left in wok or saucepan, until thickened. Stir in soy sauce and sesame-soy which will give the sauce a lovely sheen. Spoon sauce and pineapple pieces over duck. Serve with fried brown rice.

Left: Walnut Chicken (below) in Cellophane Noodles Basket (p33). Right: using 2 ladles to make cellophane noodle basket.

Walnut Chicken

Hop Tow Gai

Preparing chicken for Walnut Chicken.

3 chicken breasts
1 egg white
2 teaspoons cornflour
125 g (4 oz) shelled walnuts
2 cups vegetable oil
½ teaspoon salt
½ cup chopped water chestnuts, celery, bamboo shoots or lotus root
1 hot chilli (if desired)
¼ cup vegetable stock
1 teaspoon bean paste (min see jeung)
noodle basket

Remove skin and bones from chicken breast. Cut into 1 cm (½ in) dice and place in a bowl. Mix in egg white and sprinkle with cornflour. Deep-fry walnuts in hot oil until crisp (be careful not to burn). Drain on absorbent paper. Sprinkle with salt. Heat oil again in wok and when hot, deep-fry chicken until just coloured. Do a few pieces at a time. Remove and drain. Pour off most of the oil, which has a walnut flavour and reserve for later use. Heat remaining oil and stir-fry vegetables for ½ minute. Return chicken and cut-up chilli and mix together, stir-frying all the time. Pour in vegetable stock and stir in bean paste. Cover with a lid and cook for 1 minute. Serve sprinkled with toasted walnuts in cellophane noodle basket. See photograph above.

*Pecan nuts are a good substitute.

Fresh Lychee Chicken

250 g (8 oz) chicken meat
2 egg whites
¾ cup rice flour
2 tablespoons water
1 cup vegetable oil

Marinade
- **1 tablespoon soy sauce**
- **½ teaspoon sesame oil**
- **salt and pepper**
- **1 tablespoon rice wine**

Sauce
- **1 cup vegetable stock**
- **1 teaspoon sugar**
- **1 tablespoon lemon juice**
- **1 tablespoon cornflour**
- **1 tablespoon water**
- **12 fresh lychees**

Cut chicken meat into 2 cm (¾ in) dice. Marinate chicken for 20 minutes then coat in batter. Put egg whites in a bowl then stir in the rice flour alternately with water. Batter should be thick enough to cling to the diced chicken.

Deep-fry in oil until golden brown, a few pieces at a time so they will not stick together. Remove and drain. Pour off all the oil and keep for later.

To make sauce: heat wok again and pour in vegetable stock. Add sugar, lemon juice and cornflour blended with water. Stir until thickened then put in peeled lychees. Stir to heat and pour over chicken. Garnish with tomato.

Mushrooms with Fried Chicken

Doong Gwoo Chow Gai

750 g (1 ½ lb) chicken
oil for deep frying
½ cup soy sauce
½ cup water
¼ cup rice wine
few lengths of shallots
10 fresh mushrooms

Wash and clean chicken, taking care to remove blood clots inside carcass. Dry thoroughly. Tie string on neck for easy handling. Heat oil in wok and, holding string on chicken, ladle hot oil to brown chicken all over. (Pour off excess oil and strain for use later.)

In a large saucepan put in soy sauce, water, wine and shallots. Place chicken in mixture and simmer until tender, approximately 20 minutes (do not allow to burn). Replenish water. In the last 5 minutes of cooking add mushrooms. Serve with green vegetables.

Wrapped Lettuce Leaves

Sarng Choy Bow

1 lettuce
2 chicken breasts
1 egg white
¼ teaspoon salt
1 teaspoon cornflour
2 slices ham
6 fresh mushrooms
1 tablespoon chopped shallots
1 carrot (or choose bamboo shoot, water chestnuts, onion)
2 tablespoons vegetable oil
mix together:
- **2 tablespoons rice wine or sherry,**
- **1 teaspoon soy sauce,**
- **2 teaspoons oyster sauce**

1 cup cellophane noodles (jum see)

Crisp lettuce by washing, then soak in cool water. Cut into a 'cup' shape by placing lettuce leaf over a rice bowl. Place another rice bowl on top and cut away excess. Allow to soak in cold water with rice bowl on top to preserve the shape. Place in refrigerator to cool until ready to serve.

Remove skin and bone from chicken then chop meat into small pieces. Place in a bowl, stir in egg white, salt, then sprinkle with cornflour. Chop ham, mushrooms, shallots and choice of vegetables into same size, making a roughly-cut mince of ingredients.

Heat wok and when hot add oil. When smoking put in chicken and stir continuously but do not allow to brown. Add vegetables and rice wine mixture and cook for 1 minute. Place in a deep bowl which allows the mince mixture to keep hot. Drain lettuce and dry on absorbent paper. Spoon 2 tablespoons of mince mixture onto lettuce cup, sprinkle with cellophane noodles, wrap into an envelope shape and serve. Serves 4.

Sweet-Sour Vegetables with Chicken

Sin Tim Gai

1 carrot
cabbage
1 onion
1 capsicum
pineapple pieces
1 piece fresh green ginger
3 chicken breasts
½ teaspoon salt
1 egg, beaten
2 tablespoons cornflour
1 cup vegetable oil

Sweet-Sour Sauce
- **1 tablespoon honey**
- **1 tablespoon lemon juice**
- **4 tablespoons vinegar**
- **4 tablespoons sugar**
- **1 teaspoon tomato sauce**
- **1 teaspoon Worcestershire sauce**
- **2 tablespoons cornflour**
- **1 tablespoon water**
- **1 teaspoon sesame oil**

Shred vegetables to make up 2 cups. Remove skin and bone from chicken breasts and cut meat into thin slices. Sprinkle with salt, dip into beaten egg then sprinkle with cornflour. Heat oil in wok and deep-fry chicken until just coloured. Drain. Remove most of the oil from the wok, heat again and stir-fry vegetables for 1 minute or until limp. Stir in sauce (see below) then return chicken to mix together. Serve hot with fried rice.

To make sweet-sour sauce: heat honey in small saucepan then stir in lemon juice. Put in vinegar and sugar and stir until sugar is dissolved. Then mix into tomato sauce and Worcestershire sauce. Blend cornflour with water and stir into sauce until thickened. Lastly, sprinkle in sesame oil to give the sauce a sheen.

Master carver, Raymond Leung, at work with vegetable carvings. The Imperial Banquet was introduced during the reign of Emperor K'ang Hsi (1684 – 1707). This was a dazzling feast that lasted several days with lavish presentation and the rarest and most exotic foods. This Imperial Banquet is still continued on a smaller scale by the wealthy and the nobility, and today, a banquet to honour friends and relatives still survives – the size of which depending on the financial situation. At these functions vegetables play an important part of the decoration of the food and table. Chefs carve talismen, cranes, phoenix and animals out of carrots and turnips. Other figurines, including the Eight Immortals, are made with flour and water dough and painted.

Vegetables with Meat

Meatballs on Pastry

Kno Yuk Yin

250 g (8 oz) minced meat
1 onion, finely chopped
1 carrot, finely shredded
salt and pepper
½ teaspoon sesame oil
½ teaspoon soy sauce
20 pieces won tun pastry
2 tablespoons cornflour
1 cup vegetable oil
250 g (8 oz) soy bean sprouts, blanched
few cooked green beans

Mix minced meat, onion and carrot together. Season with salt and pepper, sesame oil and soy sauce. Knead mixture gently to adhere together. Roll into small balls 2 cm (¾ in) in diameter and seal in circles of pastry using a little water, if necessary. Roll lightly in cornflour. Heat oil in wok and when hot, roll meatballs gently around to brown and allow to cook through for about 5 minutes. Remove and drain. Serve on top of soy bean sprouts and decorate with green beans. See photograph p53.

*Won tun pastry can be obtained at oriental supermarkets.

Carrot and Turnip Casserole

Mun Lor Bark

500 g (1 lb) minced pork
1 tablespoon soy sauce
1 teaspoon sesame-soy
1 teaspoon cornflour
2 tablespoons rice wine
½ teaspoon salt
1 carrot
1 turnip
freshly ground pepper
1 tablespoon coriander leaves

Place minced pork in a deep casserole basin and blend in soy sauce, sesame-soy, cornflour, rice wine and salt. Peel carrot and turnip and cut into tiny dice. Place on top of pork mince. Sprinkle with freshly ground pepper. Steam over low heat on a trivet or rack deep enough to hold basin above water for approximately 1 hour. (Replenish water when necessary.) Garnish with coriander leaves.

*The steam generates enough moisture for this dish.

Fried Brown Rice (p75), Bitter Melon with Fillet Steak (p65) and Long Beans with Beef (p65).

1.Placing mince, spinach and shallots on top of pork caul.

Meat Roll

Kno Yuk Guern

250 g (8 oz) minced meat
salt and pepper
1 teaspoon bean paste (min see jeung)
1 teaspoon sesame-soy
½ Chinese spinach, cooked
1 tablespoon shallots, minced
1 sheet pork caul (jee mong)
coriander

Place mince in a bowl and mix in salt and pepper, bean paste and sesame-soy. Spread pork caul out on working surface and flatten mince on top in a round shape. Put chopped up spinach and shallots on top. Roll the caul round the whole mince roll, tucking in the edges. Deep-fry over moderate heat, continually basting meat roll until cooked, about 8 minutes. Drain on absorbent paper. Have deep-fried cellophane noodles spread out on serving platter. Place meat roll on top. Garnish with coriander. See photographs, left and p47.

2.Rolling caul around the mince roll.

Woolly Lamb

Fun See Yong Yuk

500 g (1 lb) lamb chops, lean
10 mushrooms, sliced
1 piece fresh bamboo shoot, sliced
125 g (4 oz) green beans, blanched
6 fresh water chestnuts (or use onion or celery), sliced
½ cup vegetable oil
1 clove garlic
1 cup stock
1 tablespoon cornflour
1 tablespoon water
1 tablespoon soy sauce
1 teaspoon sugar
salt and pepper
60 g (2 oz) transparent noodles (fun see)

Shred lamb into 5 cm (2 in) lengths and cut vegetables into similar size. Heat wok and when hot add 2 tablespoons oil and crushed garlic. When smoking, remove garlic and stir-fry lamb until just coloured. Remove and keep warm on serving platter. Add a little more oil if necessary and when hot, stir-fry bamboo shoots, green beans, mushrooms and water chestnuts together for ½ minute. Put in stock and cornflour blended with water and stir until sauce thickens. Return lamb and correct seasoning by adding soy sauce, sugar and salt and pepper. Serve on large platter on top of deep-fried transparent noodles.

To deep-fry transparent noodles: loosen noodles and deep-fry in hot oil, a little at a time. To assess correct temperature, heat oil in wok and when hot enough, a tiny length of transparent noodle will immediately sizzle and rise to the top. Remove and drain on absorbent paper. Place on serving platter, crush gently, then top with lamb.

3.Deep-frying cellophane noodles.

Asparagus with Shredded Pork

Lo Soon Jee Yuk

1 bunch asparagus
500 g (1 lb) lean pork
1 clove of garlic, finely chopped
1 tablespoon bean sauce
1 teaspoon sesame oil
salt and pepper
2 tablespoons vegetable oil
1 tablespoon cornflour
2 tablespoons water

Cut off tips from asparagus and cook standing up in boiling water until tender. (Place asparagus in a long cylinder type strainer and place in a large saucepan of boiling water. Do not cover.) Retain liquid. Slice pork into thin flat pieces 2.5 cm (1 in) long and mix with bean sauce, sesame oil and salt and pepper. Heat wok and when hot, add oil. When smoking, stir-fry pork until seared. Add ½ cup of asparagus liquid and put in cooked asparagus. Blend cornflour with water and stir into mixture until sauce thickens. Serve with hot steamed rice.

*Bean sauce has whole soy beans running through the sauce and is different from bean paste, which is a purée.

Sweet-Sour Beef Balls

Sin Tim Kno Yuk Yin

1 kg (2 lbs) minced beef
2 tablespoons minced shallots
1 tablespoon chopped coriander
salt and pepper
3 eggs
2 cups rice flour
1 cup vegetable oil
1 onion, sliced
1 small capsicum or chilli
4 slices canned pineapple
1 cup vegetable stock
½ cup vinegar
½ cup raw sugar
½ cup pineapple juice
1 teaspoon tomato sauce
2 tablespoons cornflour
2 tablespoons water

Combine beef, shallots and coriander. Season. Knead lightly then shape into 20 balls. Beat eggs and flour together to make a thin batter. Roll beef balls in batter so there is only a thin coating. Heat oil in wok and when moderately hot, lower in beef balls to deep-fry until brown. Remove and drain. Pour off oil in wok, leaving 1 tablespoon. Reheat and stir-fry onion until transparent, add sliced capsicum, cut-up pineapple and stock. Simmer for 1 minute. Mix vinegar, sugar, pineapple juice and tomato sauce together and add to mixture. Blend cornflour with water and continue stirring into mixture until sauce thickens. Return beef balls to heat through.

Barbecued Pork

Char Sui

1 kg (2 lb) pork fillets or long rashers of lean pork

Marinade
3 tablespoons soy sauce
1 tablespoon barbecue sauce (hoi sin)
3 tablespoons vegetable oil
salt and pepper
¼ cup rice wine
1 tablespoon sesame-soy
2 cloves garlic, crushed
1 piece fresh green ginger, crushed
1 teaspoon raw sugar
1 tablespoon melted honey

Marinate pork fillets for at least 1-2 hours, turning over occasionally to flavour pork evenly. Arrange pork fillets on a foil-covered rack over a baking dish that contains a little water in the bottom.

Cook for 5 minutes at 250°C (480°F) both sides, then brush on marinade, lower heat and cook both sides at 200°C (400°F) for about 10-15 minutes. Cut into oblique slices and serve with mustard or plum sauce.

*Use for other recipes calling for barbecued pork.

Slicing the spiced meats (left to right): Chinese salami, chicken liver salami and dried pork.

Placing sliced meats on top of rice in individual bowls.

Steamed Rice with Spiced Meats

Larp Mee Farn

1 slice dried pork (larp yuk)
1 pair Chinese salami (larp choong)
1 pair chicken liver salami (larp yin)
500 g (1lb) rice
Chinese parsley

Wipe dried pork, Chinese salami and chicken liver salami with a warm cloth and cut into smaller lengths, if desired.

Wash rice thoroughly and place in a deep saucepan. Cover with cold water to approximately 2cm ($^3/_4$in) above rice level in saucepan and bring to the boil. When water is evaporating and air bubbles appear on top of surface, place all the spiced meats on top. Cover with a lid and steam for 15 minutes. Garnish with Chinese parsley. See photographs, left and p28.

*Rice can be cooked previously and ladled into individual bowls. Place sliced meats on top and steam for 10 minutes.

Steamed Dim Sims

25 won tun wrappers
250 g (8 oz) pork mince
125 g (4 oz) fresh prawn meat
60 g (2 oz) pork fat
4 Chinese mushrooms, soaked in warm water for 20 minutes
1 piece bamboo shoot, finely chopped
few lengths of shallots
salt and pepper
1 egg, separated
1 tablespoon cornflour
½ teaspoon sugar
1 teaspoon sesame-soy

Trim won tun pastry with kitchen scissors to a round shape. Mince pork, prawns, pork fat, mushrooms, bamboo shoot and shallots to a very fine mince. Mix in salt and pepper, egg white, cornflour, sugar and sesame-soy. Knead the mixture together until it congeals easily. Divide into 25 portions.

Place filling in centre of pastry and twist top to enclose filling. Level bottom by standing upright on board.

Arrange on oiled bamboo steamer and steam for 15 minutes. Serve with dip sauces, soy sauce, chilli. See photographs left and p66.

*Dice pork fat, boil for 15 minutes and drain. (This method ensures that the pork fat is crisp when it cools.)

This is the genuine dim sim. If you prefer, omit the fat for health reasons. Won tun pastry can be obtained at oriental supermarkets if you do not wish to make your own.

Steaming dim sims.

Slicing beef. Bitter melon, long beans and fresh green ginger in foreground.

Cutting technique for bitter melon.

Cutting technique for long beans.

Bitter Melon with Fillet Steak

Foo Gwah Chow Yuk

3-4 bitter melons
1 small fillet of steak, finely diced
1 clove garlic, crushed
1 teaspoon soy sauce
1 tablespoon vegetable oil
1 tablespoon bean paste
1 teaspoon sesame oil
1 teaspoon cornflour
2 tablespoons vegetable oil
½ cup seasoned stock

Cut bitter melon in half, lengthwise. Scoop out seeds with a teaspoon and remove top and bottom ends. Slice finely and simmer for 10 minutes in hot water to cover. Remove, drain. Reserve liquid for stock.

Marinate beef in crushed garlic, soy sauce, vegetable oil, bean paste and sesame oil for 20 minutes. Remove, drain and sprinkle with cornflour.

Heat wok, add oil and when hot, sauté beef. *Do not overcook.* Add bitter melon and mix together. Pour in seasoned stock, cover with a lid and simmer for 5 minutes See photographs, left and p60.

Long Beans with Beef

Dow Gock Chow Kno Yuk

750 g (1 ½ lbs) T-bone steak
1 clove garlic, crushed
½ teaspoon sesame oil
1 tablespoon rice wine or sherry
1 teaspoon soy sauce
1 teaspoon bean paste (min see jeung)
½ bunch long beans (dow gock)
1 carrot
1 piece fresh green ginger, finely sliced
1 stock cube
2 tablespoons vegetable oil
½ teaspoon salt
freshly ground pepper

Remove meat from the T-bone and discard any fat and tissue. Cut meat into long slices, 4 cm (1 ½ in) x 1 cm (¼ in). Place in a bowl. Put in garlic and stir together with sesame oil, rice wine, soy sauce and bean paste. Allow to stand while preparing long beans. Snip ends of beans with scissors and cut into 8 cm (3 in) lengths. Peel carrot and cut into rounds. Place beans and carrot in wok with water to cover. Add ginger and crushed stock cube. Bring to the boil (approx. 5 minutes). Then remove beans to serving plate. Allow carrot to cook for a further few minutes to tenderize. Remove to serving plate. Pour off stock for later. Reheat wok and when hot add oil. When oil is hot, stir-fry onion, put in beef and stir-fry until seared on both sides. Return beans and carrots and season with salt and pepper Pour in ½ cup of vegetable stock (left from cooking of beans) and heat all together. Serve hot with steamed rice. See photograph p60 and left.

*The use of T-bone steak embraces 2 textures of meat; sirloin and fillet.

Stir-frying beef and long beans.

Lantern Sweet-Sour

Doong Sin Tim Loong

1 cup mixed vegetables – carrot, turnip, onion, capsicum, cauliflower, bamboo shoots, radish, gherkin, cucumber
1 tablespoon salt

Dressing
1 tablespoon raw sugar
2 tablespoons lemon juice
1 clove garlic, crushed
1 tablespoon water
1 teaspoon sesame-soy

500 g (1 lb) lean pork
1 egg
1 tablespoon soy sauce
½ cup cornflour
oil for deep frying

Sauce
1 tablespoon vinegar
½ teaspoon salt
½ teaspoon sesame oil
1 tablespoon raw sugar
1 tablespoon tomato sauce
1 cup vegetable stock
1 tablespoon cornflour
1 tablespoon water

Choose 1 cup of mixed vegetables cut into dice, small batons or shredded. Sprinkle with salt and allow to stand overnight in refrigerator. Next day rinse vegetables with cold water and drain thoroughly. Place in a jar or bowl and mix in dressing. Allow to stand for 2 hours before using.

Cut pork into dice, small batons or shred (same shape as you cut your vegetables). Place in a bowl. Mix in egg, soy sauce and sprinkle with cornflour. Deep-fry pork in wok until golden brown. Drain. Place on serving platter and keep warm.

To make sauce: pour off oil leaving one tablespoon to reheat. Stir-fry vegetables for ½ minute then mix in sauce ingredients. Blend cornflour with water and cook together until sauce thickens. Pour over pork cubes.

*This dish is presented wrapped in a cellophane lantern to trap the aroma of flavours and is a specialty of Lantern Festival time. See photograph opposite.

Cabbage Rolls

Yeah Choy Guern

10 large head cabbage leaves
5 cups hot water
½ cup vegetable oil
750 g (1 ½ lbs) minced pork
1 onion, minced
6 dried mushrooms (soaked in water for 20 minutes, then minced)
1 cup cooked brown rice
salt and pepper
1 tablespoon soy sauce
1 tablespoon bean paste (min see jeung)

Place cabbage leaves in hot water for 1 minute to limp. Drain and dry with absorbent paper. Heat wok, add oil and when hot, stir-fry pork, minced onion and mushrooms until lightly browned. Mix in rice, salt and pepper, soy sauce and bean paste. Allow to cool.

Divide mixture into 10 portions and place on cabbage leaves. Fold over in an envelope shape and secure with a bamboo skewer. Place in shallow casserole ready for steaming, approximately 30 minutes.

Chrysanthemum Vegetable with Barbecued Pork

Tong Oong Choy Chow Char Sui

1 bunch chrysanthemum vegetable (tong oong choy)
250 g (8 oz) barbecued pork (see recipe p63)
3 tablespoons vegetable oil
1 teaspoon soy sauce
½ cup vegetable stock

Cut off roots and wash chrysanthemum vegetable thoroughly, drain. If the vegetable is young, leave the separate leaves and stalks together in a small cluster. If the vegetable is too long, cut each stalk into 2 sections. Any flower buds are edible. Slice barbecued pork into 2.5 cm (1 in) lengths. Heat wok and when hot add oil. When oil begins to smoke, put in chrysanthemum vegetable and stir-fry quickly. Put in soy sauce and vegetable stock and simmer until vegetable limps, 3-4 minutes. Put in barbecued pork to heat through. Serve with steamed rice. See photograph p49.

White Turnip Salad (p36), Steamed Dim Sims (p64), grapefruit segments garnished with white turnip bird, and Lantern Sweet-Sour (above).

Inset: Chopping selection of mixed vegetables for Lantern Sweet-Sour.

Oyster Sauce Vegetables with Fillet Steak

Hor Yo Yuk

500 g (1lb) fillet steak
2 tablespoons oyster sauce
1 teaspoon soy sauce
1 tablespoon rice wine
1 teaspoon sesame oil
1 piece fresh green ginger
1 length shallot
1 length celery
1 zucchini
3 tablespoons vegetable oil
2 tablespoons stock

Cut beef into long thin slices. Marinate in oyster sauce, soy sauce, rice wine and sesame oil for 15 minutes, then drain. Scrape skin from fresh ginger and cut into wafer-thin slices. Cut shallot, celery and zucchini into small lengths. Heat wok, add oil and when it starts to smoke put in beef to just colour. Remove to serving platter. Stir-fry all the vegetables together. Add stock then return the beef to wok for a further minute.

Stuffed Mushrooms

Yeung Doong Dwoo

250 g (8 oz) pork, veal, beef, prawn, fish or a mixture of pork/veal or pork/prawns
1 slice ham fat
1 tablespoon minced onion
1 tablespoon soy sauce
1 teaspoon sesame oil
1 tablespoon bean paste (min see jeung)
1 egg
1 tablespoon cornflour
20 Chinese mushrooms (soaked in warm water for 20 mins, choose uniform size)
½ cup vegetable stock
1 tablespoon rose wine
2 Chinese salami

Mince selection of meats and add ham fat and onion. Place in a bowl and mix in soy sauce, sesame oil and bean paste. Stir in unbeaten egg and sprinkle in cornflour. Spread filling into mushrooms, packing in firmly. Place mushrooms on a deep plate ready for steaming. Pour over vegetable stock and rose wine. Cut salami into 2.5 cm (1 in) lengths and split top into 4 sections, but not completely through. Push into filling with cut side facing upwards. Steam for 20 minutes. The salami will open up like a flower.

Steamed Bread Rolls (p70), steamed rice with a carved carrot statue, Sizzling Mongolian Lamb (p70) and Cucumber and Onion Salad (p33).

1

2

3

4

Sizzling Mongolian Lamb

Moong Goo Yong

3 lamb chops, (chump)
2 cloves garlic, crushed
1 piece fresh green ginger, crushed
1 tablespoon sesame seed paste (or peanut butter)
¼ teaspoon five-spice
1 teaspoon bean paste (min see jeung)
1 dried hot chilli (or ½ teaspoon chilli powder)
½ teaspoon raw sugar
1 tablespoon soy sauce
2 onions
¼ cup vegetable oil

Slice lamb thinly and place in a bowl with garlic and ginger. Mix in another basin the sesame seed paste, five-spice, bean paste, minced dried hot chilli, raw sugar and soy sauce. Stir this into the lamb and allow to stand while you prepare the onions. Slice the onions into wedges, from top to bottom. Heat wok and when hot, add oil. When smoking, stir-fry onions until slightly brown. Remove to warm platter. Heat wok again and stir-fry the lamb a little at a time, moving to side of wok as pieces become seared on both sides.

To serve, heat sizzle plate and place onions around edge. Fill centre with lamb filling. Garnish with coriander sprig. Serve with steamed rice, a side salad, and steamed bread rolls – see recipe below. Photographs left and p69.

*Instead of making steamed bread rolls, use day-old sliced bread and steam on top of rice in last 5 minutes of cooking.

Steamed Bread Rolls

Min Bao

1 pkt dried yeast or 15 g (½ oz) fresh yeast
2 tablespoons sugar
water
1 cup milk
500 g (1 lb) plain flour

Mix yeast with sugar and warm water in a basin. Allow to stand 15-20 minutes until it doubles in volume. If using fresh yeast, crumble the yeast in a bowl. Mix in sugar and warm water. Heat milk until just warm. Sift flour in a large mixing bowl and make a well. Pour in yeast and mix together. Add warm milk gradually to make a firm dough. Knead lightly. Dough is correct consistency when it does not stick to the bowl. Grease bowl lightly, cover with a tea towel, place in warm part of kitchen and allow dough to double in bulk, about 2 hours. Knead dough again and repeat process, only leaving it for 30 minutes. Flour board and knead dough until smooth. Make into desired shapes and steam for 10 minutes. Chinese bread rolls vary in shape and design and are sprinkled with toasted sesame seeds after they are steamed. Serve with Mongolian Lamb (see recipe above).

---

1. Slicing lamb.
2. Adding seasoning to lamb.
3. Stir-frying lamb.
4. Serving on hot sizzle plate.

In a Buddhist Temple

There are many Buddhist temples and village shrines in China and Hong Kong. These places of worship are usually well maintained with meticulously polished floors, and flowers and incense being changed daily. Although Buddhists are classified as vegetarians, some include white meat and fish and oysters in their diet, but never red meat. On a recent tour of Hangzhou, China, during April, Ching Ming Festival time, my group had the opportunity of having a 12-course vegetarian banquet in the monastery. There, everything was spotlessly served and beautifully presented, and, of course, strictly vegetarian.

The Buddhists show considerable expertise in the art of vegetable cookery, mainly because they are vegetarian and the presentation of each course is a challenge. Ingenious methods are employed to group soy beans, lentils and nuts to represent and taste like meat. I have experienced some thirty such dishes at a banquet function each with its own individual taste.

One of the best-known dishes is Jie (recipe below), eaten daily, which consists of many dried ingredients which together constitute all the necessary nutrients and vitamins that your body requires for longevity. Each dried ingredient has its role to play. Some of the more unfamiliar ingredients include seaweed, beancurd, lotus, seeds, roots, barks and fungi.

The Buddhist monks welcome travellers at the Precious Lotus Monastery (Po Lin Tse) on the Island of Lantau, off Hong Kong Island, and there is also a restaurant which features vegetarian dishes.

Buddha's Delight

Jie

1 small pkt maidenhair seaweed, 60 g (2 oz), soaked in water for 20 minutes
20 dried mushrooms, soaked in warm water for 20 minutes
4 lengths dried beancurd (yin foo jook), soaked in warm water for 20 minutes
1 teaspoon vegetable oil
20 water chestnuts
½ cup gingko nuts (bark gwor), peeled
20 dried red dates (hoong joh), soaked in warm water for 20 minutes
60 g (2 oz) transparent noodles, soaked in warm water for 20 minutes
1 teaspoon sugar
2 tablespoons oyster sauce
1 tablespoon soy sauce
1 cup rose wine

All dried ingredients must be soaked beforehand to reconstitute themselves. After soaking and rinsing the maidenhair seaweed and mushrooms, place in enough water to cover and boil for 15 minutes. Reserve liquid for stock. Cut beancurd into shorter lengths, 6 cm (2 ½ in) Heat a large wok or saucepan and add oil. When hot, stir-fry water chestnuts, but do not brown, then add gingko nuts, dates, noodles, seaweed, mushrooms, beancurd and sugar together with the liquid left over from cooking the mushrooms. There should be at least 1 cup of liquid. Mix thoroughly. Put in oyster sauce, soy sauce and rose wine and simmer for 30 minutes. Replenish with water if beginning to dry – the mixture must be moist.

*Buddhist make this in large quantities at a time and eat it every day.

Cooking in the Firepot ∧

Slicing fish for the Firepot. (Mystic Knots in foreground.)

Silver Wood Ears (p76), in their dry state (foreground), and soaking in water. >

Chinese Firepot

Firepot cooking originated in Mongolia. In the north of China, firepots are cooked in a utensil with a funnel in the centre. Charcoal is used for fuel and lamb is the main ingredient.

In the south, it is known as 'Dah Bin Loo' (fire on the table) and seafood and meats are both used. Malayasian Chinese call it 'Steamboat'. But whatever it is called, it is great fun to have a firepot party. It is so much easier for the host as everything is prepared in advance. It is literally a do-it-yourself affair.

Purchase one or two firepots or use an electric wok or fry-pan, small gas ring or an electric hotplate, or a butane cooking heater. All the food – vegetables, meats or seafood – is arranged in separate dishes on the table with special dip sauces for everyone's taste. The food is cooked by the guests, with the gracious assistance of the host, who sees that each guest is catered for adequately by occasionally selecting a choice morsel with a serving pair of bamboo chopsticks.

Steaming hot stock is poured into the firepot, and hot charcoal is placed at the base on the grate to ensure that it remains at correct temperature during the meal. The selection of food is presented on large platters. Vegetables and meats are already washed and cut up into lengths easily handled by the cooking chopsticks. Each guest takes a piece of food, holds it in the boiling stock, cooks it according to individual taste and then dips it into one of the sauces to enhance the flavour. Boiling stock is replenished and when cooking is finished, the balance of food is cooked and the soup is served – by this time it is absolutely delicious. Steamed rice is served and the meal is completed by serving a dessert or fresh fruits.

Firepot – Northern Style

lean lamb
fresh vegetables in season
transparent noodles
fresh beancurd
Seasoned Stock

or

prawns
chicken breast (cooked)
bamboo shoots
mushrooms
transparent noodles
tiensen cabbage

Firepot – Southern Style

Dah Bin Loo

fish fillets
crab sticks
shallots 'mystic knots'
lettuce
transparent noodles (soaked for 10 minutes then boiled for 10 minutes)
fresh vegetables in season
Seasoned stock

or

prawns
bor choy mushrooms
transparent noodles

***To make mystic knots: take 1 shallot, trim root end and outer withered leaves. Place in warm water until limp (approx. 15 mins). From root end, fold up end in 5 cm folds, then twist top half around centre of folded portion then tuck end inside.**

Legend of Joong

One of the festivals on the Chinese calendar is the Dragon Boat Festival, held on the Fifth Moon, the most important event of summer. It is a time to pay respect to ancestors and to appease the Dragon, Controller of the Waters. Every festival has its own food speciality and for this occasion it is joong. Legend has it that Ch'u Yuan, a Minister in the 4th century BC, was so frustrated with the Emperor who was displeased with his reforms that he threw himself into the river. All efforts to save him were in vain, so the people threw rice in the water to appease the hungry ghosts. As the fish ate up all the rice the people had to find another method to prevent this happening so joong was designed. The rice was wrapped in lotus or specially selected leaves tied with a piece of silk with five colour threads; red, yellow, blue, black and white. Today the joong is tied with twine and the stuffing inside is usually glutinous rice, mixed with beans, pork and eggs, or just vegetables mixed with the rice. They are wrapped in triangular or long shapes, then boiled for 3-4 hours. Today, as these cakes are so popular they are made in all shapes and sizes and sold all the year round.

Sticky Rice Dumplings

Joong

1 kg (2 lbs) glutinous rice (nor mei fun)
2 teaspoons salt
125 g (4 oz) fat pork (with streak of lean meat desirable)
dried lotus leaves
length of twine
6 salted ducks' eggs
250 g (8 oz) soy beans, soaked overnight

Wash rice and soak for about 2 hours in enough water to cover. Pour off excess water and mix in the salt. Dice pork into 2.5 cm (1 in) pieces, sprinkle with salt and allow to stand overnight. Soak lotus leaves in hot water to soften. Sterilize the twine by placing in boiling water. Separate yolks from the egg whites, and only use the yolks. Place rice and beans together in a large bowl and mix together.

Using 2 or 3 lotus leaves, make a cone shape and spoon in 4 tablespoons of rice mixture, press in a cube of pork; then 2 more tablespoons of rice mixture. Press in the egg yolk, 2 more tablespoons of rice mixture, then press in another cube of pork. Close with another lotus leaf and tie the whole dumpling with twine. Boil in a generous amount of water for 3-4 hours.

Reheat next day and simmer for 1 hour. To serve hot, untie the lotus leaves and cut dumpling into slices with clean twine, or when cold, untie the lotus leaves and cut dumpling into slices and dip into beaten egg. Fry gently in hot oil on each side until golden brown. Serve with sugar if desired.

Spicy Brown Rice

Heung Wong Farn

2 onions
1 cm (½ in) piece fresh green ginger
1 garlic clove
¼ cup vegetable oil
500 g (1 lb) brown rice
½ teaspoon five-spice
2 petals star anise
1 large tomato
3 cups water
3 cups ground almonds
1 tablespoon coriander leaves

Mince 1 onion, ginger and garlic together. Finely slice the other onion and fry in vegetable oil until golden brown. Set aside. Wash rice and place in rice cooker or large saucepan with five-spice. Add mixed onion, garlic and ginger. Put in star anise and sliced tomato, together with 3 cups of water. Bring to the boil, cover with a lid and simmer until rice is tender. Mix in ground almonds. Serve rice in a deep bowl sprinkled with fried onions and coriander leaves.

Fried Brown Rice

Chow Wong Farn

1 tablespoon vegetable oil
1 egg
barbecued pork (recipe p63)
3 cups cooked brown rice, cold
½ cup stock
1 teaspoon soy sauce
2 tablespoons chopped shallots
salt
freshly ground pepper
bean sprouts

Heat wok and when hot add oil. Beat egg lightly and make into omelette. Remove, and when cool, cut into small pieces. Cut up barbecued pork to make up half a cup. Reheat wok, add brown rice and stock. Stir-fry continuously for 15 minutes over moderate heat. Pour in soy sauce, add pork and shallots, return egg and cover with a lid and heat through for 2 minutes. Adjust seasoning to taste by adding salt and freshly ground pepper. Sprinkle with bean sprouts and serve. See photograph p60.

*To test when wok is hot enough, a drop of water will sizzle immediately.

Vegetable Rice Pancakes

1 kg (2 lbs) fresh rice flour pastry (sar hor fun)
2 tablespoons vegetable oil

Vegetable Filling
1 small onion, shredded
1 carrot, shredded
1 cup cabbage, shredded
1 stalk young celery, shredded
1 cup bean sprouts
1 tablespoon satay sauce
1 teaspoon bean paste (min see jeung)
salt and pepper
1 tablespoon chopped coriander
2 tablespoons toasted sesame seeds

Soy Sauce Dip
½ cup light soy sauce
½ cup vegetable oil
2 teaspoons sesame-soy

Lay rice flour pastry out on working board and cut in 13 cm (5 in) squares. Heat wok, add oil and when smoking add onion, carrot, cabbage, celery and stir-fry for ½ minute. Then add bean sprouts, satay sauce and bean paste and mix to heat through. Correct seasoning. Allow mixture to cool and drain off any liquid (there should not be much moisture remaining).

Divide mixture into number of pastry squares required and squeeze mixture to firm. Roll up to form an open-ended long shape. Place rolls, seam-side down, on a lightly oiled plate or aluminium round disc (specially available for this purpose) and steam for 10 minutes. Sprinkle with toasted sesame seeds and garnish with extra coriander sprigs. To serve, spoon over soy sauce dip.

To make soy sauce dip: put soy sauce in basin. Heat vegetable oil and add to soy sauce. Mix in sesame-soy.

*The aluminium round disc is part of the equipment that accompanies bamboo steamers.

Baked Rice Cup Cakes

Mei Beang

1½ cups glutinous rice (nor mei)
1 cup white sugar
1½ cups water
½ cup self-raising flour

Wash rice, cover with water and soak overnight. Rinse and drain. Put rice in a blender with sugar and water and blend until very fine. Pour into mixing bowl and stir in flour. Divide mixture into small casserole dishes and place in steamer. Steam for 20 minutes. Test by inserting a bamboo skewer in centre – if it comes out clean, the cup cakes are ready. Remove from casserole dish and allow to cool.

*Alternatively, cakes can be baked in moderate oven for 15 minutes. Cover securely on top, so result will be a pale cup cake.

Beancurd Fritters

Tao Fu Beang

6 blocks fresh beancurd
1 onion, finely chopped
120 g (4 oz) wholemeal flour
60 g (2 oz) brown breadcrumbs
1 teaspoon mixed herbs
1 teaspoon soy sauce
1 tablespoon cornflour
1 cup corn oil

Drain moisture from beancurd and blot between absorbent paper. Using chopsticks or fork, mash beancurd in a bowl. Mix in onion, wholemeal flour, breadcrumbs, herbs and soy sauce. Knead the mixture gently to bind it together. Shape into small balls then flatten into fritter, 2.5 cm (1 in) in diameter. Sprinkle with a little cornflour.

Heat wok and when hot add oil and fry fritters on both sides over moderate heat until golden brown. Drain on absorbent paper. Delicious hot or cold.

Gluten Steaks

500 g (1 lb) gluten flour
½ cup soy flour
1 x 7 g (¼ oz) pkt active dry yeast
1 tablespoon soy sauce
2 cups water
8 cups seasoned vegetable stock
1 cup breadcrumbs
1 cup vegetable oil for deep-frying

Mix gluten flour and soy flour together in a bowl. Sprinkle with yeast. Mix soy sauce with water and mix into flours to make a stiff dough. Knead lightly. Turn out on board and roll out into small lengths to resemble slices of filet mignon. Cook in vegetable stock for 30 minutes. Drain on absorbent paper. Sprinkle with breadcrumbs and fry until golden brown on both sides.

Pumpkin Rolls

2 tablespoons margarine
2 tablespoons sugar
1 egg
½ cup pumpkin, cooked soft
4 cups wholemeal flour
½ teaspoon salt
1x 7 g (¼ oz) pkt active dry yeast
1-1 ¼ cups water

Cream margarine and sugar together. Beat in egg and mix in pumpkin. Sift flour and salt together and place in a bowl. Mix in dry yeast. Make into a dough with creamed mixture and water. Shape into a long roll and cut into 12 pieces. Make either round or oblong. Place on an oiled tin and allow to rise until doubled in bulk. Brush the top with a little water, then bake for 20 minutes in moderate oven 180°C (375°C).

*Served hot in North China during the cold months.

Fresh Fruit for Dessert

Sen Gwor

apple (Delicious)
watermelon
pineapple
black grapes

Cut apple into 6 wedges. Cut a 'v' out in centre of apple wedge. Cut through skin at remaining 2 points almost to end of wedge. Soak in cold water for 15 minutes. Cut 6 wedges of watermelon. Cut pineapple into 6 pieces. Add a few black grapes. Arrange decoratively on platter, then place in refrigerator to cool for 1 hour before serving.

Silver Wood Ears Dessert

1 pkt (25 g) silver wood ears
5 cups water
1 cup white sugar
1 can mandarin oranges

Rinse silver wood ears in cold water, then cover with hot water and soak for 20 minutes. Remove the hard stem and drain. Put silver wood ears in a saucepan with sugar and stir until sugar dissolves, then simmer for 30 minutes or until tender. Place in refrigerator to cool. Serve chilled with mandarin orange segments or any choice of fruits. Add ice cubes in summer. To serve hot, add fruit after cooking.

*This is considered a tonic food for good health, keeping your body young and healthy. See photograph p72.

Dip Sauces

Easy Sweet and Sour Sauce

Sin Tim Jeung

½ cup sugar
¼ cup vinegar
1 teaspoon salt
1 cup water
1 tablespoon ketchup
1 teaspoon Worcestershire sauce
2 tablespoons cornflour
2 tablespoons water

Place sugar, vinegar, salt and water in saucepan and slowly bring to the boil. Stir in ketchup and Worcestershire sauce and cook in cornflour blended with water, stirring until thickened. Cool and store in a jar for future use.

Chinese Vinaigrette Sauce

Salat Jup

2 tablespoons lemon juice or white vinegar
2 tablespoons sugar
2 cloves garlic, minced
1 teaspoon sesame-soy
½ teaspoon salt
1 teaspoon chilli sauce
½ cup vegetable oil

Mix lemon juice and sugar together and pour over minced garlic. Add sesame-soy, salt and chilli sauce. Mix in vegetable oil and blend all together. Especially delicious with seafoods.

Home-Made Oyster Sauce

4 dozen raw oysters
3 cups liquid from the oysters
½ cup soy sauce
2 tablespoons rice wine
½ teaspoon salt
2 teaspoons cornflour
1 tablespoon water

Put oysters in a blender (chop finely) and place in a saucepan. Add oyster liquid. Bring to the boil, then simmer for 15 minutes. Strain through muslin cloth. Stir in soy sauce, rice wine and salt. Blend cornflour with water and stir through sauce to thicken. Place in a sterilised container and keep in refrigerator. Use as a seasoning sauce.

Home-Made Five-Spice

20 clusters star anise
4 whole sticks of cinnamon
2 tablespoons Szechwan peppercorns
2 tablespoons cloves
3 tablespoons fennel

Blend all the spices together in an electric blender until reduced to a powder. Keep stored in an air-tight container.

Barbecue Sauce

1 onion
2 cloves garlic (minced)
4 tablespoons vegetable oil
2 tablespoons mustard
1 cup raw sugar
1 cup water
½ teaspoon five-spice
½ cup tomato paste
1 teaspoon salt
1 teaspoon chilli powder
2 tablespoons soy sauce
½ cup lemon juice

Heat wok and when hot add oil and stir-fry onion until limp, but do not brown. Add the balance of ingredients in the order listed above. Simmer until all are blended together, stirring continuously. If too thick, add a little more water. Adjust seasoning to individual taste – too hot, reduce chilli; too sweet, reduce sugar.

Fresh Green Ginger Dip

Geung Yo

185 g (6 oz) fresh green ginger
1 teaspoon salt
½ cup vegetable oil
1 teaspoon sesame-soy
1 tablespoon chopped shallots

Peel and grate ginger and form into a mound. Mix salt into grated ginger and pour in warmed vegetable oil and sesame-soy. Serve a tablespoonful in an individual saucer, and sprinkle with shallots.

Chilli Oil

Lart Ju Yo

4 red capsicums
2 red hot chillies
1 teaspoon salt
1 cup vegetable oil

Cut up capsicums and chillies very finely. Add salt and oil. Simmer for 10-15 minutes. Strain and retain oil.

Satay Sauce

1 cup crunchy peanut butter
1 tablespoon sesame-soy
1 tablespoon lemon juice
½ teaspoon curry powder
1 teaspoon raw sugar
½ teaspoon salt
½ cup vegetable oil
½ teaspoon seasoning (stock cube) dissolved in ½ cup water
1 chilli, finely chopped
1 tablespoon bean paste (min see jeung)

Place all the ingredients in a small saucepan and stir continuously over moderate heat, until thoroughly mixed together. The oil will rise to the top. When cool, store in a sterilised jar until ready for use. Spoon some of the paste and the rich top oil together when adding to your dish.

Sauces – Individual Serves

1 tablespoon soy sauce
¼ teaspoon sesame oil
¼ teaspoon vinegar
¼ teaspoon sugar
1 teaspoon rice wine or sherry
1 teaspoon minced white end of shallots
……

1 tablespoon oyster sauce
1 teaspoon hot vegetable oil
½ teaspoon sesame oil
1 teaspoon minced coriander
……

1 teaspoon chilli sauce
1 tablespoon hot vegetable oil
½ teaspoon sesame oil
1 teaspoon minced shallots
½ teaspoon soy sauce
……

1 tablespoon grated fresh ginger
¼ teaspoon salt
1 tablespoon hot vegetable oil
……

1 tablespoon soy sauce
1 teaspoon sesame oil
1 tablespoon hot vegetable oil
¼ teaspoon mixed mustard
……

1 tablespoon hoi sin sauce
1 tablespoon hot vegetable oil
1 teaspoon sesame oil
……

1 tablespoon sesame paste or peanut butter
1 teaspoon hot vegetable oil
½ teaspoon soy sauce
1 teaspoon rice wine or sherry
……

Glossary

The Chinese terminology is given in the Cantonese dialect, the most frequently spoken by overseas Chinese, and I have endeavoured to simplify the spelling by phonetic equivalents to help when purchasing ingredients. Chinese names sound quite different, depending on the dialect spoken, although the Chinese characters remain the same.

BEANCURD

Fresh beancurd (Tao Fu)
This can be purchased in small blocks 6 cm ×6 cm (2 ½ in ×2 ½ in) square and it is relatively inexpensive. It is used in vegetarian dishes, is easily digested and very nutritious being made from purèed soy beans. It has a delicate burnt flavour and when added to other foods absorbs the flavour of that dish. Use as soon as possible as it is extremely perishable. Will keep refrigerator for a few days by changing the water.

Dried beancurd sticks (Yin Foo Jook)
This is a by-product of the soy bean and has a glossy appearance. It is in a long stick form, 25 cm (10 in) long, folded to make a double stick. It needs to be soaked for at least one hour before use, and broken into short lengths. This is a very good quality beancurd and is very necessary in vegetarian dishes where it is braised and used in soups.

Dried beancurd sheets (Foo Jook Pin)
As above, but made into flat sheets. It is very resilient and will keep its texture when added to other foods. Used for braised and soup dishes. The very thin variety is used as a wrapper of other foods. Available in package form.

Red beancurd (Narm Yue)
This small 2.5 cm (1 in) block is preserved taro root which has been purèed, seasoned, fermented and coloured red on the outside. It is used in braised and long-cooked dishes and imparts a very rich flavour. It is also available in all-white blocks which are used as a relish with steamed rice. Available in cans and jars. Keeps up to three months in the refrigerator.

BEAN PASTE (Min See Jeung)
This is a salty dark brown paste made from black soy beans and spices. Excellent for all types of dishes. It is available in jars, either semi-whole beans or purèed. Yellow bean sauce has sugar added.

BEAN PASTE, SWEET (Tim Jeung)
This is a sweet paste made from Chinese red beans, sugar and spices and is dark reddish-brown in colour. Available in cans and jars and can be stored in the refrigerator for up to three months.

BLACK BEANS (Dow See)
This seems to be everybody's favourite addition to beef and crab. They are available dried and in cans. The dried ones need to be washed thoroughly and then placed in a small bowl. Pound them with the top end of a cleaver and marinate in rose wine or brandy.

If using the canned variety, there is no need to wash, but use very sparingly as they are salty. Different varieties are black and yellow. They keep 2-3 weeks if removed from the can and placed in an airtight jar in the refrigerator.

CELTUCE (Woh Sun)
Rarely available outside Shanghai where the long, thick, stem is pickled and canned. If available fresh, use as for Chinese broccoli (gai larn).

CHINESE CRAB APPLE (Sarn Jar Beang)
A small thin red disc, available in packets. It is eaten as a sweet but when dissolved in hot water is added to sauces, especially sweet and sour, to give additional colour and flavour.

CHINESE SAUSAGE (Larp Cheong)
These are small pairs of sausages tied together with string with pork or chicken liver filling, both sweet and salty. They are steamed and can be added to other dishes. Available by weight at oriental delicatessens. Also known as wax sausages.

CLOUD EARS
See Fungi.

CORNFLOUR
As this is found in most kitchens I have used it in most recipes requiring a thickening agent It is easy to use and gives excellent results. When sauces need to be thickened just blend the cornflour with cold water and cook into the dish to remove the raw taste. Other starches which give good results include arrowroot, tapioca, rice, potato and chestnut. Do not use wheatstarch as the sauce will be opaque and heavy. Cornflour is also known as cornstarch.

DRIED SHRIMPS (Har Mei)
Tiny dehydrated peeled shrimps which are used in soups, steamed eggs and other dishes to give added taste. Wash and soak before using to soften. They are finely ground and are often used to sprinkle on top of food in lieu of crab roe (which is becoming difficult to obtain).

FIVE-SPICE (Heung Lo Fun)
A blend of spices consisting of aniseed, cloves, cinnamon, anise herb and the aromatic seeds of fennel. Use only a small amount each time. There are different brands with different amounts of the spices in the blending, resulting in a slightly different taste and aroma. The original blend was considered the classic of them all.

FUNGI, CLOUD EARS (Chee Yee, Mook Yee)
Small pieces of black, wrinkled fungi that need to be soaked in cold water for 20 minutes when they will expand at least four times in size, resembling a beautifully formed ear. They have a crinkly texture and an elastic-like quality to absorb the flavours of richer foods. Especially good in soup. The larger variety, mook yee, is also a tree fungus and is used in soups for medicinal purposes because of the protein, calcium, phosphorus, iron and carbohydrate content. In their dry form they will keep indefinitely stored in an air-tight container. They are available in small packages, sold by weight. See also White Clouds.

GINGER (Geung)
Fresh green ginger is one of the most important ingredients in Chinese cuisine. It adds a particular flavour to food, especially seafood as the Chinese believe that it has the quality to disguise the 'sung', fishy aroma. It is also a delightful addition to meat and vegetables. I purchase one 'hand' at a time and just leave it in the kitchen. Sometimes the tiny shoot at the tip blooms – this piece is deliciously tender. One needs only to break a piece off the ginger then scrape the skin and shred or crush as desired. Some prefer to store ginger in a screw-top jar, fill it with dry sherry and place in the refrigerator. In my recipes I refer to 'a piece of fresh green ginger' – this piece should be about 2.5 cm (1 in) long. When making ginger sauce, especially for white chicken, you use greater quantities. This is considered one of the classic sauces of southern Chinese cuisine.

GINGKO NUTS (Bark Gwor)
These small, soft-shelled pointed nuts are white with a brown skin. They have to be blanched to remove the brown skin before use and are quite soft. They have a delicate flavour and are used in soups and braised dishes. Available fresh (need to be shelled) or already shelled in cans.

GLUTINOUS RICE (Nor Mei)
Also called 'sticky' rice. It is a short grain, opaque rice that is sticky when cooked so is ideal for Chinese cakes and pastries. Especially good when wrapped in lotus leaves. It is more expensive than ordinary rice, and each grain is heavier in weight. Very rich in vitamin B. Always soak 1-2 hours before cooking.

GOLDEN NEEDLES (Gum Jum)
These are the dried stems of the lotus plant and are pale gold/brown in colour. They have a distinct flavour and are an interesting addition to any dish. They are always part of vegetarian dishes. Can be tied into a 'mystic knot' as an added decoration to any dish. Available in packets and shelf life is up to 6 months.

HOI SIN SAUCE
Chinese barbecue sauce. It is very spicy, made from soy beans and spices, sweet or hot, according to the brand, and is a thick dark red/brown sauce. It is used for extra flavouring of all foods and especially for spreading pancakes that accompany Peking Duck. Available in cans or jars. Store in refrigerator.

LONG BEANS (Dow Gock)
These green beans measure up to 90 cm (3 ft) in length and there are two varieties, dark green and light green. The narrow pods are considered more succulent and more crunchy. Select beans that are uniform in diameter. Chop into lengths and cook as for green beans. A good substitute for snow peas or green beans.

LOTUS
Every part of the plant is utilised. The seeds (nuts) of the lotus flower (lin jee) are removed along with the bitter embryo, and cooked. The rhizomes are used for food and the starch is removed and used as a thickening agent. The stems (gum jum) are used in vegetarian dishes. The leaves, which are large, are dried and used as wrappers for steamed foods. The root (lin kno) is used in soups and braised dishes. It is peculiar as it has lots of tiny threads which are part of the sap. It has a holey flesh which creates a lacey pattern. It is cooked, sliced and candied for the New Year. Available fresh, sold by weight, and in cans.

MANDARIN SKIN (Gom Pei)
The skin of the mandarin is cut into four sections leaving the bottom part intact so that the skin falls away in one piece. The best skins come from the large, flat, brightly coloured fruit. The skins are threaded on twine and allowed to dry in the sun for one week and then kept in an air-tight container until ready for use. It is used in long-cooked dishes, soups and steamed dishes.

MUSHROOMS
Chinese mushrooms (Doong Gwoo)
These winter mushrooms are always dehydrated and used prolifically in Chinese dishes. They must be soaked before use when they will expand to their original size. They are brown to black in colour and come in varying thickness and size, the thick centres are considered the best. These mushrooms which grow on trees, have been cultivated for more than 1000 years. When choosing these mushrooms, choose those that are completely dry and look underneath to see that there are no signs of damage by insects. Store in an air-tight container. Sold by weight.

Winter mushrooms are flavoursome and succulent and do not disintegrate while cooking. Another variety is shaped like a flower with its distinctive 'petals'.

Straw (Tso Gwoo)
These mushrooms are so-named because they are cultivated on rice straw. They are very firm when young, grey to brown in colour, and darken in colour with age when the mushrooms grow through the top of the membranes that enclose them.

Helmet
So called because they have a shape resembling a 'helmet'. Available in cans. They are soft in texture and only need to be heated through and added to a dish.

Champignon
Small, round, smooth mushrooms, also known as 'button' mushrooms. Available in cans. Use immediately upon opening as they deteriorate very quickly if allowed to stand. All fresh mushrooms must also be used quickly as they are very perishable.

OYSTER SAUCE (Hor Yo)
This sauce has a thick dark brown consistency and the genuine variety is made from oysters, soy sauce and added spices. It is used for flavouring meats, poultry and seafood. Usually sold in bottles and is available in larger quantities in cans.

PLUM SAUCE (Mui Jeung)
Different brands of the Chinese plum sauce vary slightly in flavour because of the quantities of plums, apricots and chilli used in the recipe. Try them all and select your favourite to use as a dip sauce for roast meats and poultry.

PORK NET, CAUL FAT (Yee Mong)
This is a lacy sheet of fat from the omentum and is used to wrap food before steaming or deep-frying. It dissolves in the hot oil when deep-fried but lends considerable flavour to the food it wraps. Available in oriental supermarkets already frozen in sheets and will keep for a week in the refrigerator.

RED DATES (Hoong Joh)
Dehydrated dark red dates in different sizes. Used in soups and steamed dishes. Gives a delicious individual taste of sweetness.

RICE NOODLES (Sar Hor Fun)
These have an opaque appearance and are made from rice and corn. They are usually 1 cm (¼ in) wide when dehydrated and folded together in stick form. Soak in water for 15 minutes to uncoil. Used in soups and braised dishes, never deep-fried. Fresh rice noodles are available in rolls and sheets at oriental delicatessens and can be cut into desired lengths.

RICE PAPER (Mei Jee)
Edible transparent sheets made from glutinous rice and used to enclose savoury and sweet food. Can be used as a spring roll skin. Available in plastic packs ready for use and need to be moistened slightly with a warm cloth before use so as to make them pliable.

RICE WINE (Mei Jeou)
Chinese rice wines are readily available under different labels. The rose wine is amber in colour and has a high alcohol content. Japanese rice wine (saki) or its by-product (mirin) can be substituted. Always served warm in small cups. Using sherry, either sweet or dry, does vary the flavour of the particular dish. The northern Chinese usually sprinkle rose wine on to dishes just before service, similar to 'flambè' in the western world.

ROCK SUGAR (Bing Tong)
These are amber-brown sugar crystals used for sweets, cakes and sugar syrup and to glaze poultry. It does not tend to be oversweet, and must be dissolved before use. My sister and I loved to eat it as rock candy when we were children. The Chinese in Hawaii colour it red, green and yellow for decoration.

ROSE WINE (Mui Gway Lui)
There is no substitute for rose wine regarding flavour. This high alcohol content wine imparts an exotic quality to food, especially in a vegetable dish. Use in marinades for meat and poultry.

SEAFOOD STICK (Hoi Sin Tu)
It is a small roll of minced seafood, coloured red on the outside, and is used as a substitute for seafood in all kinds of dishes.

The Japanese make a larger roll, often with colour through the inside, and when cut into slices it makes very attractive patterns; mainly used in soups, it is called *kamaboko*.

SEAWEEDS
(Chee Choy)
Very fine black threads of dried seaweed used in fasting dishes by Buddhists.

Maiden's hair (Fatt Choy)
Fine black hair-like dried seaweed. Soak for one hour, rinse and boil for 10 minutes and then add to vegetable dishes.

Laver
A deep purple, wafer-thin dehydrated seaweed available in 20 cm (8 in) sheets folded in half. Needs to be held over a flame to crisp slightly before use. Makes a nice contrasting pattern when rolled between ingredients or can be shredded and added to soups and salads.

Nori
Japanese name for dehydrated seaweeds, flat and coil varieties.

Dried seaweed (Hoi Di)
Broken up pieces of seaweed (processed) which only need to be soaked in warm water for 10 minutes to reconstitute and expand. Add to soup and salads.

Dehydrated seaweed
Available in large sheets and added to stock pots for extra flavour. All seaweeds are rich in iodine and minerals.

SESAME PASTE (Jee Mar Jeung)
This is a highly concentrated paste made from sesame seeds. It is available in jars or cans and needs to be used sparingly. A very good substitute is finely ground peanut butter.

SESAME OIL (Jee Mar Yo)
This is a highly flavoured oil made from sesame seeds. It is used sparingly for an added taste sensation.

SESAME SEEDS (Jee Mar)
These are used in the manufacture of cakes, candies, jams and pastries. To toast for desserts, just heat a wok, add white sesame seeds, move seeds around and toast to a golden brown colour. Keep a watchful eye on the sesame seeds and have a lid ready to place on top, as the seeds will jump around when they are ready. Available in white, brown and black varieties and sold by weight.

SESAME-SOY (Jee Mar See Yo)
This is a blend of both sesame oil and soy oil. It is a very refined oil and adds tons of flavour excitement to your dishes. I have experimented with this oil in recipes for this book and find it delicious; it is not as strong in aroma as pure sesame oil.

SHALLOTS (Choong)
All parts of the shallot are used in Chinese cooking. In Asia, shallot bulbs (choong tow) are deep-reddish bulbs that grow in clusters and are stronger in flavour than the more common white bulb. They are used extensively in all curry dishes and are especially delicious with curried chicken.

SHRIMP PASTE (Harm Har)
This purplish paste is made from tiny shrimps and it takes thousands of them to make one 400 g (14 oz) bottle. It has a strong fishy odour and one has to acquire a taste for it. Use very sparingly. Serve as an appetiser in a small dish steamed over rice while cooking.

SNOW PEAS (Hollan Doe)
These translucent green pea pods are a special delicacy. The whole pod is eaten, just remove the tips and any strings. It requires very little cooking to retain flavour, colour and vitamin content. They are also available frozen but lose their crispness in the cooking process as they tend to soften. They are also sugar-coated for Chinese New Year as a special sweet.

SOY BEAN SPROUTS (Dai Knar)
Sprouted from the soy bean and have a yellow bean at the end. The shoot should be clear, crisp and white. One of the most nutritious and economic of foods with a high protein value.

SOY SAUCE (See Yo)
The Chinese cuisine would not be as it is without the use of this ingredient. Generally available in three weights; for light cooking purposes the thin variety, *sarng chow,* is always used, then there is the medium type, a little darker and thicker and used for dip sauces and for marinating food. The third variety, *lo chau*, is thicker and darker and is used for slow cooking when extra colour and flavour is desired. The best quality is made through natural fermentation and then allowed to age.

STAR ANISE (Bart Gock)
An eight-petal, deep brown, star-shaped herb used for dishes needing long cooking times. Has an exotic flavour and haunting aroma. It must be used sparingly otherwise it has a tendency to overpower the flavour of the dish.

SWEET POTATOES (Farn See)
There are many varieties of sweet potatoes, with light brown skin, red skin and orange skin. The orange-fleshed ones are sweeter and more nutritious than the white-fleshed types.

SZECHWAN PEPPER (Foo Jew Fun)
A very fragrant reddish-brown peppercorn from Szechwan. Sometimes prepared roughly crushed with toasted salt and pepper added. This condiment can be overpowering, so use with discretion.

WHITE TURNIP (Lo Bark)
A long white turnip with smooth skin. The vegetable can be eaten raw or cooked and when grated is used in savoury puddings. Scrape skin then cut into pieces, chunks, slices or grate. Use for soup – it withstands long periods of cooking without disintegrating.

WHITE CLOUDS (Bark Chee Yee)
A cultivated fungi, similar to cloud ears, only white in colour. It needs to be soaked in water for at least an hour before use. Used in soups, sweets, vegetarian dishes and prized for its medicinal qualities. Available in dehydrated form and sold by weight.

Standard Measures

The metric weights and liquid measures used in this cookbook are those of the Standards Association of Australia. Imperial weights are given in brackets.

Abbreviations used

gram	g	ounce	oz
kilogram	kg	pound	lb
millilitre	ml	inch	in
centimetre	cm	foot	ft
millimetre	mm		

New Zealand, American and Canadian weights

These countries use metric measures that vary slightly from those of Australia, as shown in the table below. None of the recipes in this book will be significantly altered if the Australian measures are used.

Country	*Cup*	*Tablespoon*	*Teaspoon*
New Zealand	250 ml	15 ml	5 ml
America	237 ml	14.9 ml	4.9 ml
Canada	227 ml	14.2 ml	4.74 ml

Conversion of Dry Ingredients

Avoirdupois	*Metric*	*Avoirdupois*	*Metric*
½ oz	15 g	11 oz	345 g
1 oz	30 g	12 oz	375 g
2 oz	60 g	13 oz	410 g
3 oz	90 g	14 oz	440 g
4 oz (¼ lb)	125 g	15 oz	470 g
5 oz	155 g	16 oz (1 lb)	500 g (0.5 kg)
6 oz	185 g	24 oz (1½ lb)	750 g (0.75 g)
7 oz	220 g	32 oz (2 lb)	1000 g (1 kg)
8 oz (½ lb)	250 g (0.25 kg)	48 oz (3 lb)	1500 g (1.5 kg)
9 oz	280 g	64 oz (4 lb)	2000 g (2 kg)
10 oz	315 g		

Conversion of Liquids

Imperial	*Metric*
1 fl oz	30 ml
2 fl oz (¼ cup)	60 ml (¼ cup)
3 fl oz	100 ml
4 fl oz (½ cup)	125 ml (½ cup)
5 fl oz (¼ pint)	150 ml
6 fl oz (¾ cup)	185 ml (¾ cup)
8 fl oz (1 cup)	250 ml (1 cup)
10 fl oz (½ pint)	315 ml (1¼ cups)
12 fl oz (1½ cups)	375 ml (1½ cups)
14 fl oz (1¾ cups)	440 ml (1¾ cups)
16 fl oz (2 cups)	500 ml (2 cups)
20 fl oz (1 pint)	625 ml (2½ cups)

Metric usage follows Metric Conversion Board Recommendations.